Eating the ELEPHANT

A true story of loss, betrayal and abuse

Alice Wells

D0757257

Mirror Books

Published by Mirror Books,
an imprint of Trinity Mirror plc,
1 Canada Square,
London E14 5AP, England

www.mirrorbooks.com
twitter.com/themirrorbooks

Mirror Books Editor: Jo Sollis
Design: Julie Adams
Editor: Charlotte Cole

ISBN 9781907324611

12 11 10 9 8 7 6 5 4 3 2 1

First paperback edition printed and bound in Great Britain
by CPI Group (UK) Ltd, Croydon, CR0 4YY

* All names, places and identifying details have been changed.

Front cover image: Trevillion Images

To family and friends you have been my strength when

I was uncertain how to carry on.

To my father, who will never know how grateful I am that

he taught me the beauty and power of the written word

and its ability to transcend matters of the broken heart.

To my children, you are amazing, courageous and

beautiful, and your resilience knows no bounds.

I love you beyond words.

Alice Wells

Contents

Introduction

*'There is no greater agony than bearing an untold
story inside you'*
Maya Angelou

Before you venture into the pages that follow, I feel
compelled to issue a health warning. I urge you to take
reasonable protective steps in order that you are equipped to
enter what is, in emotional terms, a hard-hat area.

For most of us pornography and paedophilia are not
subjects that readily present themselves as casual dinner
party topics – at least not in any normal world – and
thankfully most of us will never encounter its presence
anywhere near our lives or those of our loved ones. However,
many of us have been guilty of assuming that this
unspeakable addiction is confined only to the darker recesses
of society. But this is wrong. This silent predator has, for too

long, successfully hidden itself in plain sight within all levels of our society.

For those whose lives have been personally impacted, its effects are intense and far-reaching. A child victim will often carry the imprint of their abuser long into their adult life. At its core it is paralysing and isolating, the collateral damage is immense.

It has taken Alice almost seven years to write her story. She has thought long and hard about whether she should write it at all – it is not easy to digest.

How, you may ask, does a young dedicated doctor, a devoted mother of two and wife of nine years, come to terms not only with the sudden death of her husband, but with the terrifying discovery that the man she fell in love with and thought she knew had been living a double life? He was a paedophile.

Add to that the thousands of miles standing between her and her much loved family, the woeful lack of compassion and understanding from police, teachers, health professionals and counsellors, the growing fears surrounding her own small children, and we find a woman utterly alone; fighting for survival inside a living nightmare.

You may feel a range of emotions while reading this book. Outrage, horror, sadness, helplessness and compassion are just a few. I encourage you to give voice to them. Step back, allow yourself the space to acknowledge your response and release it. Silence is deadly.

Then – I urge you to read on . . .

Why? Because you will discover a strength and beauty that rises gracefully out of this desolation. You will discover a deeply sensitive, compassionate, professional woman and friend who, despite all she has endured, not only remains alive, but has a quiet, firm hope for the future. The honesty with which Alice shares her story is testament to her inner strength and tenacity. She allows us in to her darkest moments and her deepest fears. She trusts us with the agony of her grief and loss. It has cost her much to share this pain with us. We owe it to her to read on.

But not only her, for Lisa Marie and the thousands of beautiful, innocent and vulnerable children whose young bodies are, and have been, so hideously used and discarded in the pursuit of personal and collective gratification of the worst kind. We owe it to them.

And it is ultimately for them that Alice writes. We dare not ignore her.

Lifecentre exists for such as these. Lives that carry the indelible stain of sexual abuse are welcomed through our doors. Broken, fearful hearts find their way nervously onto our helplines on a daily basis. There, the untold stories are finally told. We count it a privilege to walk with them as they take what are in many cases the first, tentative steps towards getting their lives back. And it is possible – truly.

As you read on you will sense from time to time how the enormity of this story overwhelmed Alice. But it is not a story of shame and hopelessness, it's a story of perseverance and patience; of gratitude for friendship; a story of grace. She has much to teach us. At the centre is a thread – what do you do when your worst fears about what happened to your family turn out to be true. How do you cope? You exist in the presence of an unspeakable reality: a societal taboo which is also fraught with heated opinion. There is an elephant in the room. You fear a gut-wrenching repulsed response from others which showers you with shame. Those who do know are at a loss for words. You create two versions of yourself: the respectable widow and the secret wife of a paedophile who longs to break free and shout about the injustices of the deal that life has thrown at her. You want to scream that this is so unfair. But you don't. And for Alice, in the middle of this mayhem, a loyal friend poses a wise question: How DO you eat an elephant?

Sue Mills
Lifecentre – supporting the survivors of rape and sexual abuse

Prologue

Invite the image in, he tells me, in his quiet but confident voice; sit with this elephant a while. I hesitate, uncertain in the promise that this beast of an image can be tamed at all; its power diminished by familiarity.

It is cold in the room. The delicate young girl stands next to a bed, sparsely covered with a cheap comforter; she is separate from the two men. Even in the half-light that is struggling to break through a small crack in the dense brown curtains, I can see her goose bumps on bare skinny arms. 'Little Miss Sunshine' beams a smile from across the chest of her brightly coloured t-shirt. I stop; thinking of my own daughter, seven years old with the very same shirt in our wardrobe at home. With a reticent smile, I recall how on our last family holiday, she had excitedly darted around our hotel room. With boundless energy she had thrilled at bouncing on the bed. She was so keen to explore every nook and cranny.

Not this girl. She has not moved. She is rooted to the sticky stained carpet of this dingy motel.

My heart beats faster and my palms are moist as I draw her in. My throat is dry and my head foggy. My chest tightens and I struggle to breathe. Must I speak? Must I allow my mind's eye to have its voice? He waits to hear; to guide me through. It will help he says.

One of the men moves to behind a camera. It is set up on a tripod in the far corner of the room. The zoom is poised and ready to fire the shots. The other moves toward the girl and tells her to undress; slowly. I know she has been here before, and follows the routine. They practiced at home. The man with the camera, and a kind smile, tells her to stop. She has removed her t-shirt. The one who is closest to her takes it in his sweaty hands and folds it neatly, placing it on a chair; sunny side up. It is all she can do not to wrap her arms around her; it feels so cold. Click, click, flash.

My attention is drawn to her greying schoolgirl knickers, which droop loosely around her narrow hips. On demand, she drops them to the floor. They hang there around her skinny ankles, as if for eternity. Click, click, flash.

Tears begin to fall. They are mine not the girl's. He does not pass me a tissue to stem the flow. Tears will caress the rigid cracks which have formed in my soul; they are a necessary lubricant. Her face does not betray her emotions. She is gone. All that is left in the room is her fragile shell. Where does she go, I wonder?

I want to run. Surely, we are done here. I need to come up for air. But the elephant remains seated on my chest. I gasp. I am suffocating under its weight. I push the thoughts and images back down inside me; they can't be spoken. The words will instead gather much later, on a page, and even then they are stifled by my sense of propriety.

Later, I can see the man with the camera and the kind smile. He sits encircled by a desk; his monitor screen providing the only light in this basement room. A silence hangs in the air and passes up the stairs, wrapping itself around those sleeping on the floors above. Smiling, he leans back in his broad black leather office chair, his senses alert, he is satisfied with himself. In one hand he holds a technical pencil; systematically, he writes her name, followed by a number: Lisa Marie 0001. She is ready to upload.

NOTES TO SELF
Instructions for Eating an Elephant

VITAL STATISTICS OF AVERAGE ELEPHANT
Weight up to 6300kg
Height 330cm
Skin thickness 2.5cm

Characteristics
Strong sense of family and death; very protective of each other; share similar emotional traits and behaviours with humans, including compassion, envy, jealousy, happiness, sadness, tantrums and the ability to grieve deeply; they are known to sleep standing up at times.

You will need
A team
Tenacity
Courage

Wisdom
Patience
Sharp implements
A very small spoon
Space
A vision

Instructions

This elephant is unlikely to surrender easily. Once she has been brought to the ground, wait for the elephant to fall silent. And clear a space. Do not try to tackle the whole thing alone. You will be worse off for doing so. You will find that small pieces are far easier to digest. Warning: elephant meat can be a major cause of indigestion in larger portions. Regurgitation may occur. But do not worry; if you follow these simple instructions and have your tools to hand you will manage even the greatest of elephants. And when complete, its sad and hollow shell will remain to remind you how far you have come.

CHAPTER 1

A Fairy-tale Beginning

June 1997

'CARDIAC ARREST, Cardiac Arrest Trauma Room Bed 2 Accident and Emergency ... bzzzz ... Cardiac Arrest ...'

The shrill voice cuts through the air in the dark refuge of my on-call room. It is 5 a.m. The bedsheets are still cold and the pillow plump. Moments earlier, just before the arrest call came in, I had been filled with hopeful expectation of a few hours' sleep. It was not to be. My 'sleep total' on this night would be measured in minutes not hours. I grab my white coat, its bulging pockets weigh me down with the essential novice doctor toolkit: stethoscope, tendon hammer, pen torch, drug handbook, notebook and the pocket guide to medicine (920 pages). There is no hustle and bustle in the corridors at this time of day. Silence fills the many corners of the hospital. All you can hear as I come to life are tired and heavy feet pounding the corridor. I take a moment's breath and join my bleary-eyed team at the bedside.

There is no pulse. We begin the manoeuvres. My hands push firmly down on the chest of this cold young body: a woman in her early thirties. Her clothes now lie torn in tatters about her flailing limbs. Someone searches desperately for a vein. I count for the team and the minutes tick by. One and two and three... Her face is drained of colour and there is no response to our desperate attempts to revive her heart. Arms get tired and the resuscitative cycles feel futile. Any sign of life has long departed. She had wanted to die. A large dose of b-blocker had provided the answer she was looking for. She is blue. We call it. Time of death: 6.36 a.m.

My shift has come to an end and I walk away from this casualty into the freshness of a spring morning. I did not know her name. Grasping a warm takeaway cup of coffee, I now lean on the effects of caffeine as it begins to circulate and revive my jaded self, just enough. I don't want to think too much; I am running late for my train to the airport. A week of leave starts this morning. I am officially on holiday.

I desperately needed a break. House year, as a junior doctor, was taking its toll. It was a test of stamina which I imagine is akin to army boot camp: a repetitive exercise in sleep deprivation, and in physical as well as emotional survival, with routine long hours. I had not planned to go on my own to Egypt. It was a spur of the moment decision. Perhaps, a moment of crazy impulse purchasing: I needed an adventure that was completely different from the kind of adrenaline rush I had found on the wards. One dreary Saturday afternoon, sleep deficient after being on-call all night (I was about to clock over a hundred hours of work that week), I had crawled into town. With a degree of determination, I'd made my choice from the last-minute-break notices and the glossy photographs in the travel agent window and booked my holiday escape. Egypt looked warm and exotic; the four-star hotel was a far cry from the grey concrete of the hospital residence; and this 'special offer' holiday provided a bargain for this newly-qualified doctor.

Just a week later, I found myself walking alone through Cairo airport, stunned by the sight of guards with enormous rifles hanging from their belt handles. A minibus transported me from the airport through the dusty Cairo streets to another world. It was just eight hours since I had been running to that cardiac arrest call where the young woman had died. I could still see her chilled blue lips and fingertips as I collected my suitcase from the airport baggage conveyer belt.

The Cairo Hilton hotel exuded elegance and luxury. I was more used to the gloomy damp-ridden digs of hospital accommodation, of dripping sinks and the noise of fellow inhabitants intruding through paper-thin walls. I had perhaps found my escape. The cool marble entrance adorned with a large sparkling crystal chandelier stood in stark contrast to the muddy streets and chaos just outside, where heat, dust and noise were all consuming. Set back from Cairo's main commuter route, the hotel sat in the shadows of the famous Giza pyramids and Sphinx. I watched amused and astonished at the feast for my eyes, nose and ears: donkeys, minibuses, taxis, cars with missing doors and seats, ancient carts, bicycles and people chaotically stood six or more deep as five million commuters jostled throughout the day with Cairo's own inner-city population. Shouts, car horns, bells and heehaws created a deafening symphony. The heat cooked the smells of car exhausts, animal waste and roadside fruit stands. In this commuter belt, it is a miracle that the pyramids have survived and are so accessible; sitting at the edge of such commotion. My romance with Egypt had already begun. I had discovered a city so rich to the senses: where better to fall in love?

I crossed the street taking my life in my hands; recklessly naive, I wanted to explore. It soon became clear that Cairo was not a destination for the faint-hearted single girl. No willows or wallflowers would survive unaccompanied in this melting pot. In just a week, I do not exaggerate or jest, I received four marriage proposals and counted an equal number of adventures. I was not used to this level of mishap or male attention, and I certainly didn't think I had courted this in any way in my dress or my attitude. My week's holiday was already feeling quite surreal even before I met Mark.

He treasured our first encounter. Indeed, Mark clearly remembered his first sighting of me. I had rushed down to the hotel lobby fresh out of the shower, my wet long hair was dripping on the polished marble floor. I had wanted to make the deadline for booking a trip to Alexandria. It had sounded adventurous and romantic: a bus across the desert, a visit to an ancient first Christian site, a walk along the beach of a seaside resort and a chance to visit another of the Seven Wonders of the World, the lighthouse at Alexandria. I booked my seat and hurried back to my room to change for dinner. I didn't stop to notice the American tourist who was also standing at the desk. Mark followed suit and booked the trip for the following day. He was sufficiently intrigued to contrive a meeting with this seemingly unaffected British girl who was oblivious to the puddle forming at her feet on the glossy marble floor. Inadvertently, I had left a lasting impression and a romantic chase had begun.

The next morning, as the golden sun rose over the pyramids, our group of seven boarded a small minibus, in the company of our toothless but unashamedly flirtatious tour guide. We were an amusing collection of souls. A very English conservative married couple, a flamboyant detective and his wife (who had been reluctant to leave the poolside sun lounger for the far less alluring desert), a flapping older gay man dressed as if he had walked off the set of a Merchant Ivory film, a smooth-talking American serviceman and me: a vulnerable young female English doctor desperately dressed to be less conspicuously different in a long tunic, straw sunhat and headscarf. I perhaps looked like I needed to be rescued.

We hit the full impact of Cairo's commuter traffic in the early heat of the day and within a few minutes of joining the main highway through the desert, encountered our first drama. We were pulled over by an unmarked police car, containing two men bearing heavy rifles. The bus driver was asked to present all of our passports and his driving credentials, these documents were scrutinised and we were advised they would need to be taken to the police station for further inspection. Our driver's own papers were not up to date. An animated conversation in Egyptian followed, which was eventually translated: unless we paid a bribe we would not be permitted to continue our tour. Our penniless driver turned to his tourist cargo for help. He was unashamedly apologetic for this unanticipated diversion. We were framed into turning over a collective sum of several hundred Egyptian pounds: a small fortune to our bandits but a small change inconvenience to the tourist cargo. The money paid and an amicable bon voyage in Egyptian exchanged between conspirators, we continued on our way with little further fuss except a collective sense that we had been duped; by both our driver and the police.

Leaving the boisterous rich landscape of Cairo, and reaching forward into the desert, a bland overstretched canvas lay in front of us which seemed to go on for miles beyond the horizon. Two hours later, hot and thirsty, we eventually stopped at a roadside rest station, a pit stop in the middle of the desert which provided little shelter from the disabling heat of the sun and shifting dust storms of the sand. At this virtual oasis, Mark and I first met. We had only exchanged glances from either end of the minibus up until now. I had of course taken stock of him and observed that he was charmingly friendly with the other passengers. I had watched how the gay man in particular seemed drawn in to his company. I too was intrigued by our fellow traveller.

I emerged from the rather rustic ladies to hear a gentle whispering call for help from the American in our party. In our brief roadside repose, Mark had found himself in the midst of another drama: an insistent but somewhat bedraggled Egyptian man was making advances on Mark as he stood waiting to reboard our bus. Feeling outnumbered and unsure of how to dodge a further kerfuffle, Mark asked if I had any suggestions. I immediately threw my arms around him to give him a hug, whispering that this unwelcome admirer might back off if he thought we were together. It worked, much to our relief. As we climbed back into the relative safety of the bus something new had begun.

After this icebreaker, we found each other's company infectious, we laughed, shared stories and experiences and stole knowing glances, almost to the exclusion of all our fellow tourists. As I was herded around the wondrous lighthouse at Alexandria by a large group of young Egyptian men who seemed both fascinated by and desperate for western flesh, Mark had the opportunity to repay his debt by protecting me. These men were seemingly intrigued by the pallor of my skin and the glimpses of my long brown hair under my cautionary hat and scarf; guided perhaps by their misconceptions of what a western woman might provide. Matters of attraction were seemingly throwing Mark and I together. We found ourselves to be objects of desire in this foreign land, attention neither of us was used to.

Lunch was not an ideal romantic introduction. As the only vegetarian, in the absence of what we think was a casserole of donkey meat, I was faced with a huge plate of plain but oily spaghetti. Our restaurant sat in the hillside overlooking a rather charming small cove. This was framed with rows of coloured beach huts, set up like stadium seating just above the sand. The hectic activity on the sand below created a fortunate diversion from the embarrassing journey of slippery spaghetti from my dinner plate to my mouth. Hundreds of bathers had gathered with their sun umbrellas in one small patch of sand only a few metres square, to the point that they were practically sitting on top of each other. Rather like the chaotic capital commute, Egyptians at the seaside seemed oblivious to each other's personal space. How different they were from any northern European civilisation where queues, marking your pitch and observing a particular etiquette were expected standards for behaviour. Absurdly, just beyond the cove, a few metres away, there was an expanse of straight untouched sand which wound around the bend of the coastline. We could not understand why this small section of beach was so coveted. Trying to apply some logic, I can only assume that this was the public area and the expanse beyond was a private beach which only belonged to those who could afford the tariff. Egypt was most certainly a country of contrasts and extremes: a rich tapestry of contradictions in gold and dirty brown threads.

Acutely aware that I had just a few days remaining in Egypt, after this first meeting Mark and I were eager to spend every moment we could in each other's company. We started to get to know each other. Mark was stationed with the US air force in England, and had lived just outside Oxford for seven years. He and his family were nomadic Americans, moving from state to state throughout his childhood before settling in the South. His parents were older, and although he had happy early childhood memories of scouts and junior baseball league, as a teen he had been unsettled and lost. Often left to his own devices without parental guidance, he had fallen into the wrong crowd. He wanted to belong but, as the red-headed kid, the opportunities were narrow and the popular kids cruel. So, two worlds were opening up for him: computers and, uncomfortably, the role of sidekick to his brother Jack and Jack's friends. They entered a world of crime, drugs and fast cars; Mark was the fall guy. The military had straightened Mark out.

I stood in contrast to his world. I came from a small town in

England. I was a 'good girl', devoted to my parents, appeared bookish and applied myself to my studies at school. I could never be described as a rebel and my adventures were of a different kind. I shared with Mark my stories of being a trainee doctor, and dreams of becoming a cancer specialist. But, in my own way, I shared that overarching teenage sense of not fitting in. I came late to dating and boys. I stood apart from the popular set at school and I too had been bullied for being different.

We discovered that we both enjoyed travel and between us life had afforded us the chance to enjoy visiting some amazing places. Mark had been in Berlin when the wall came down; I had volunteered in Africa; we both loved Italy. Ironically, we had synchronously booked this crazy trip at the last minute: just the weekend before. Mark had nearly chosen Israel. We had come very close to not meeting at all.

Mark seemed insatiably romantic and chivalrous. He had military neatness and manners, and was keen to leave a lasting impression. Laughter and adventure characterised our final days in Egypt. He made me laugh. Our shared adventures added to the romance of it all. A hotel bus driver attempted to sell first his daughter, then his wife to Mark on a short journey to the Egyptian museum and then, failing that, he tried desperately to offer himself in the deal; it is no wonder we felt safer as a couple in Cairo.

Perhaps our closest scrape came the night before my return home. Mark treated me to a curry at a nearby luxurious colonial-styled hotel. We had a lovely evening and were both dreading my departure back to 'the real world' the next day. As we walked back through the poorly lit, dusty dirt streets late in the evening, a Bedouin trader cornered us in a narrow alley with his sales pitch for carpets and exquisite perfumes 'for the lady'. Mark, not wanting to offend him and interested in the stories this man began to tell, agreed to follow him into his nearby bazaar.

The long narrow front room was cocooned in richly coloured carpets, and sheer drapes enshrouded a smaller room beyond in a veil of mystery. Eastern spices and fragrances hung thickly in the air, creating an exotic atmosphere. The Bedouin told us of his aspirations to send his daughter to an American college but lamented at his abject poverty. He lavished adoring praise of the opportunities America offered his child; to him it was a promised land. A skilled storyteller, he continued with tales of his humble beginnings in the deserts beyond Cairo with his own tribe of people. Encouraged by his captive audience, he moved on to a political speech and delivered an eloquent and passionate monologue about the injustices of the Egyptian government and how his people, the Bedouins, had been marginalised.

After some considerable time had passed, I am sure he was confident that he had won our sympathies with his plight: he began his hard sell. Within minutes, we lay pray to his dealing. The atmosphere in the room changed. No longer were we being charmed by this cunning salesman, instead his tone became more menacing. Suddenly, we felt very vulnerable and shared a sense that something terrible might happen to us. I held onto Mark's hand tightly as we were lured into the back room of the shop. It was here that the Bedouin's bribes took on a new life and the true character of his threats emerged. We quickly realised how foolishly naive we had been to step off the tourist trail. We began to cautiously reverse our steps, moving as a couple, trying to stretch ourselves closer towards the lobby of his store. Our lucky break came when this wily man lost a grip on his plan; he stepped into the rear shadows of his shop to find tea for his visitors. And then we ran, as if running for our lives. We did not dare look back until, breathless, we reached the safety of the lobby of our very western hotel. In that moment, exhilarated by our shared adventure, we kissed.

Back then at the hotel, and in the months that followed, we did not stop to contemplate the complications a transcontinental relationship brings to the table. We did not consider how we would make it work. Mark was soon redeployed back to the USA. Our relationship grew at a distance. We fell in love with being in love. And two years later, I moved continents for him and for us.

The Peace of the Wild Things
When despair for the world grows in me
and I wake in the night at the least sound
in fear of what my life and my children's lives may be,
I go and lie down where the wood drake
rests in his beauty on the water, and the great heron feeds.
I come into the peace of wild things
who do not tax their lives with forethought
of grief. I come into the presence of still water.
And I feel above me the day-blind stars
waiting with their light. For a time
I rest in the grace of the world, and am free.
Wendell Berry

CHAPTER 2

A Life Less Ordinary

Sometimes I think this story is bigger than me. It still feels like it happened somewhere else in someone else's life. And yet I know this not to be true for at times it still has a pervading power to consume my every thought.

In all honesty, life ceased to be ordinary when I made that fateful decision, in 1999, to move to America. And yet the start of this day in July 2007 couldn't have been more ordinary, for it was so like any of those other days living in America that had preceded it.

My youngest child, Joseph, was eight months old and I was battling hard to keep breastfeeding while working full time. This meant getting up at 5.30 a.m. so that I would have time to nurse him before leaving for work at 7 a.m. I would tiptoe around, hoping not to wake anyone; fearing that if I did wake the rest of the house, I would not be able to finish the task.

Mark, my husband, now a master's student, was asleep in

the basement of our three-storey home. This had become the norm. Each morning, a feeling of building resentment and anger would creep beneath my skin. I would feel the weight of working full time, keeping house and being a mother. I am a bit of a perfectionist and there was always a tension; the feeling that I could not possibly be doing any of these tasks as well as I would have liked. The energy it took to even feel 'good enough' was stifling. We were not a 'team'.

By the time I had dressed and concealed the tale-tell dark circles under my eyes as best I could, Joseph was crying and ready to get up. The fifteen minutes that followed were my favourite part of the morning. My bond with Joseph had become a balm in such difficult times. As he nestled in to me, any tension was released; tears would often roll down my cheeks as I thought of the bittersweet reality I was living.

Mark had left the air force in 2003 and decided to retrain in IT. Then life dealt us a blow. When he was in the final term of his IT degree, Mark struggled with severe episodes of low back pain. While I was away for a conference in 2005, Mark collapsed unable to walk and an MRI a few days later showed a tumour at the base of his spinal cord. In the following months, he spent many hours studying in the basement, unable to sleep in our bed because of pain; he worked into the early hours.

Our focus became getting through the months to his finals and preparing for a major operation. It drew us together. Mark became emotionally more vulnerable at this time, talking for the first time about his fears of being in a wheelchair if the surgery was not successful. Delaying his surgery so that he could complete his degree, Mark eventually graduated, had a terrifying six-hour operation and made a full recovery.

Mark rarely paid me a compliment, and so I was touched
when that summer he told me he had never seen me more
beautiful than when I cared for him in the days following his
surgery. He felt treasured that he had risen to the top of my list
of priorities, something he rarely felt; such was his true
vulnerability.

That autumn, with the trauma behind us, Mark embarked
on an MBA and began to look for a job. Meanwhile, I had
successfully applied to finish my general practice training in
the UK – taking a six-month sabbatical from my American
position as insurance for the future to be able to work in either
country. After a hellish summer, my eldest child, Grace, and
I left for Britain, but Mark and I seemed closer as a couple,
pulled together by this period of adversity and vulnerability.
I was not worried about being apart for nearly six months.
We survived longer periods before. We were both thinking of
our future.

But then things really began to go wrong. One weekend
before I left for England, Mark brought home three new
computers; he had found a contract position and needed the
data space for his new employment. New accounts and
network security were created at home. He gave each of us a
password protected profile for the first time. I had neither the
interest nor the skill to understand the secure network Mark
told me he was building in our basement. My only observation
was that the network seemed to demand escalating amounts
of his time to install and then repeatedly, and quite counter-
intuitively to me, to wipe each computer clean and start all
over again. Mark's work schedule felt unpredictable and his

relationship with his new employer seemed intense, evasive and confrontational. Mark assured me that they were building a new business and this was part of the course. Invitations for me to meet his new boss, Skip, were cancelled at the last moment. Less than three months into his contract, Mark was abruptly let go.

On the phone to me in England, he would focus conversation on his evening MBA studies or Grace and my adventures, and he was able to conceal his unemployment for three months. When we returned, he excused this deception by saying he was protecting me due to the extenuating circumstances: my father had been diagnosed with lung cancer.

We had been perhaps at our happiest when Grace was born. Mark had graduated his bachelor's degree with the highest honours and our baby provided much joy. I recall Mark's delight as Grace turned around in my very pregnant belly to a torch he was shining through my taut skin; our desperate attempt to rectify her breech presentation. We were each simultaneously thrilled and overwhelmed by our new role as parent.

But it was different when I was pregnant with Joseph. We were together again but there was much on the horizon to tear us apart. As well as the pregnancy, my career was blooming but my father seriously ill. To say I was distracted from my marriage understates reality. I needed Mark's support but instead he recoiled from what to him was an affront from all he found threatening. Mark did not do 'loss' or 'dying' and I felt very isolated.

The birth of Joseph and the needs of a new-born baby and a

pre-schooler consolidated the drift that had occurred in our relationship. I was so busy balancing motherhood, being a daughter and working full time that I did not have time to miss Mark. After my father died, and I began to emerge from the initial emotional numbness, I longed to be held. I began to feel guilty that I had neglected Mark's physical needs and apologised. It was only a few months later that he casually replied: 'I don't need you; I have found other ways to satisfy myself.'

Mark's apparent sources of respite were mentorship meetings out of town, meetings for group work and late-night classes in the computer lab. He began going out of his way to help fellow students with their coursework. When he came home, he would briefly join our bedtime routine with Grace. She would giggle as Daddy read the bedtime story using his catalogue of funny voices. These precious moments would defuse my building resentment and disillusionment with what our married life had become. Then he would disappear into his basement office to toil on the computer.

Although he had agreed to move back to the UK with me at some point, he was generally distant and unhelpful. We argued a lot.

This July morning followed our usual routine: I called through Grace's door 'time to get up' and begin getting Joseph dressed. It usually took several attempts to get Grace moving in the mornings, not unusual at the tender age of four.

I could hear Mark downstairs in the kitchen. This was a little unusual as he normally remained in bed until we were about to leave. In my heart, I was hoping he might be making me a cup of tea and filling bottles of milk ready to take to nursery. But when we all arrived downstairs, he was in fact eating a 'Hungry-Man' ready meal at the counter. As a self-confessed healthy eater, how those frozen meals riled me. There was no tea and only a row of empty bottles in sight. At this point I was late: my 7.30 start began to seem unreachable. Perhaps reading the rising tension, Grace was still only half-dressed, Mark offered to take Joseph and Grace to nursery. As I packed Joseph's bottles for the day, we decided that Mark would cook and prepare a casserole for that evening's meal. I was irritated that I had to give him a detailed account of how to do this; after all I was running late and the directions are on the packet of the casserole mix.

I had been working for six years at the university hospital as a hospice and palliative medicine doctor. The colleagues I had there were my life's blood. Tears and sweat cemented us together. Although, my job was inherently stressful and emotionally intense, I derived great satisfaction from my work. It felt like a great privilege to accompany the patients and families we cared for at such difficult times in their lives. On this particular day, I was the consultant on the inpatient palliative and comfort care unit (PCCU), and it was exceptionally quiet, just three of the twelve beds were filled. I had been on-call the previous week and for the weekend, so these quieter periods were a respite, an opportunity to refill the emotional batteries, have time to 'pump' breast milk for Joseph and catch up on my patient discharge summaries.

That afternoon, I was due to go to the post-mortem of a fifty-four-year-old patient; I had cared for her during her final hours the previous week. It was an emotionally charged case

where I was trying to be an advocate for justice for her family.
I had promised them that we would try to understand why she
had died as she did. Her life had been cruelly cut short by an
overwhelming blood infection, liver and kidney failure all
following her routine dialysis treatment. Significantly, three
other patients had died that week in the same dialysis unit.
It seemed that the information available pointed toward
negligent practice. This was the first post-mortem I had
attended since my training. It was a luxury to have the
time to go.

Arriving in the basement mortuary, I had forgotten how
stark these proceedings could be: organs in plastic sandwich
boxes brought out one by one for inspection. I was struck by
the names of the dead listed in non-permanent marker on the
white board. How impersonal this aspect of care becomes, for
the families we looked after, and for me, it had all become
intensely personal. I could not help but think of Dad as I
looked at the names of the dead and the pieces of my patient
in those cold plastic containers. My throat went dry and a
grief-sized lump rose up from my chest as I tried to swallow
back the tears. After the stark white and aluminium counters
and the insipid smell of formaldehyde, I was relieved to walk
out into the brilliant sunshine. I felt the warm sun on my skin
and thought what a beautiful day it was. There was not a cloud
to be seen in the brilliant blue sky. Life could feel good.

As I returned to my office, I realised I had missed a phone
call from my mum; distracted, I had forgotten that she was
due to ring me that afternoon. Feeling awful that I had missed
her, I phoned home to ask Mark to call her and ask her to try
again. It was a difficult time for our family, not only were we

still grieving the death of my father, but my aunt was having chemotherapy for lymphoma and my grandmother, crippled with arthritis, was struggling to live alone in her home, falling several times a week. The thousands of miles between our two continents divided my heart.

I could not reach Mark at home or on his mobile and felt very frustrated. Fortunately, my mum called back, only to tell me that both my aunt and grandmother had fallen that day. I felt so angry I punched the desk in frustration. A very silly thing to do and completely out of character; a tender bruise along the edge of my hand reminded me of this later. Physical anger really is not my thing.

The ward was very quiet that afternoon but my colleague covering the rest of the hospital had been very busy with several new patients. I offered to help. I went to the surgical intensive care unit where our trainee doctor, Lara, was seeing two new patients. Both were desperately unwell. They, like many of our patients, were dying on ventilators, holding on by a thread to life. The second gentleman had been in hospital for several months and had no family. There was no one to help guide decisions about his care. As the afternoon unfolded, it became apparent that the work remaining was complex and going to take a lot longer than I had anticipated. The latest I could leave to collect the children on time was 5.15 p.m. As five o'clock rapidly approached, I began to leave a series of messages for Mark to ask him to collect the children from nursery. He was usually very good at answering the phone; my job was demanding and I could often be late.

I could feel resentment and anxiety welling up inside as I tried to balance the tension and tasks: helping to transfer two very ill patients, supervising Lara and clock watching, acutely aware I may have to leave to get our children before long. Finally, after another desperate phone call to home and Mark's mobile, I gave up at 5.35. In a flurry of apologies to Lara, I dashed off to my car to collect Grace and Joseph.

The sky was no longer blue, a storm had come in and there was a change in atmosphere that was dark and ominous. There was a palpable pressure change in the air. The heavens opened as I crossed the street to the car park and it began to rain in torrents. The traffic was at its worst. My journey home at rush hour was always awful but on this day it was exceptional. By now adrenaline was pouring out of me. The radio announced an accident at the next exit on the interstate with traffic tailing back to the university. Desperate, I took the back road home. Now I felt sick with anxiety: I was going to be late. The rain poured down and I could barely see through the windscreen. It seemed everyone else had decided on this back route too and the traffic remained painfully slow. We were all trying to beat the storm home. I tried Mark's mobile again, pleading with him to return my call and collect the children.

Where is he? How can he be so selfish? What is going on? I tried to make sense, in the desperate forty-five minutes that followed, of where and what Mark could be doing. Perhaps he had left his phone at home and was collecting the kids: silly me! Still stagnant in the traffic at 5.55 p.m., I phoned the nursery to say I was on my way but stuck; if they saw Mark could they ask him to call me. They must have thought it strange.

Finally, with just two minutes to spare before my children

were hauled up in the lobby, their parents fined, I arrived at
the nursery drenched by the unceasing torrential rain.
I grabbed a towel from my car boot to try to keep Joseph dry.
I remember I was wet through by the time I entered the front
doors; really soaked to the skin, my light cotton blouse
clinging to me. I looked a state. Embarrassed, I shrugged off
the fact that Mark had not been in, joking that he was missing
in action to Amy, the nursery manager. I dashed down to
Grace's classroom, where she was the last child waiting. We
collected Joseph, who was screaming because they had held
off giving him a bottle or food in case I wanted to do that at
home. Wrapped in towels to keep them dry, I bundled the
children into the car. By now I was fuming. Where is Mark?

As we pulled down into our steep sloping driveway, Mark's
car was not in its usual place and the electric garage door was
wide open. An office chair sat in the middle of where I would
usually park and the door into the house stood ajar. What is
going on? I shot out of the car, its engine still running, to move
the chair. By now, I was afraid and my heart began to feel like
it might jump out of my chest.

Leaving the children in the car, I briefly stepped inside the
house. In Mark's basement office it looked like a bomb had
exploded. There were cables and paper everywhere. I could not
make sense of what I could see. Had we been burgled? I closed
the office door to conceal the mess within, and I gathered up
the children. We climbed up the dark basement stairs into the
light of the open plan kitchen, living and dining areas. The
kitchen was virtually untouched – but looking through to the
living room and beyond, cables and papers were strewn across
the floor, and the house was in disarray.

I worked hard to appear calm, but I was breaking inside.
Grace asked where Daddy was and I replied that I didn't know.
'Perhaps he had a meeting or a quick errand to run,' I said,
desperately thinking on my feet.

I tried to do what was needed: feed the children. I pulled out
a microwave meal for Grace and warmed a bottle for Joseph.
I noticed that the cooking pot and casserole mix were sitting
on the counter, undisturbed from their position that morning.

Hyper-vigilant, all my senses were firing on adrenaline,
I listened out for the sound of Mark's car. By this time I was
pacing the kitchen as I gave Joseph his bottle. As I tried to
encourage Grace to eat, my eyes caught sight of the papers on
the kitchen table for the first time. It was a search warrant
from the federal court.

As I scanned the pages, the words overwhelmed me. I started
to panic – although in English, the sentences made no sense.
Tears began to stream down my face, I could not contain them
any longer and suddenly I was struggling to breathe. A little
voice reached through the fog – 'Mummy, where is Daddy?'
– and then to try to reassure me, as she saw my tears, Grace
repeated my words: 'I'm sure Daddy will be home soon
Mummy; what a silly Daddy. Perhaps he forgot he had a
meeting or something?'

My eyes returned to the paper in front of me, where the
printed words said 'child pornography'. I couldn't comprehend
the first, entirely focusing on the word 'pornography'. I felt
helpless and very scared as I looked around the mess of
the house.

Desperate, I phoned my closest friend, Clare. I am sure I

made very little sense. She was out at a restaurant having a family dinner with her children and husband. She stepped outside to talk and asked me to read the top of the papers, but by now I had shut down into panic. All I could do was shake and let the tears flood out of me, as I held Grace and Joseph in my arms. In silence, we clutched onto one another and time stood still, for just a moment.

Not much time passed before Clare and another friend, Kate, arrived to take control. I broke down in their arms, filled with fearful questions: 'Where is Mark?' 'Are we safe?' 'What happened at my house this afternoon?' Kate took Joseph and Grace upstairs, as Clare and I tried to make sense of what we could see. We had not been burgled but searched by the police ...for pornography. We began our own search. It took me some time to realise they had taken all of our computers and cameras, and most of the DVDs, videos and other photographic equipment. Cables were strewn everywhere. Eventually, our eyes fell upon a business card left on the kitchen island; it was for a postal inspector, Jack Hutton.

I was later to learn that the US Postal Inspection Service (USPIS) was a federal law enforcement agency that prevents crimes that affect the US Mail. This was the first time I'd ever heard of them.

Concealing myself on the stairs down to our basement, I tried to call Inspector Hutton's mobile number; there was no reply, of course: it was after 5 p.m. I left a message: 'I found your business card in my kitchen. I am desperately trying to find out what has been happening at my house today; and my husband is missing.' Then I called the city hospitals: ERs, admissions – maybe Mark had been in an accident. I called the police station and the county jail. I explained, 'My husband is missing ... maybe he has been arrested?' Fearful, I did not reveal the fragments I knew of the story so far.

There was no trace of him; no word anywhere. Surprisingly, no one asked any questions. I was in a state of terror as I made these calls in the dim light. Like a fugitive below stairs, I hid because I was fearful Grace might overhear these distress calls.

Next, I tried Mark's mobile phone again. Now my gaze was drawn to the flashing light of the answerphone: no one had retrieved my earlier calls to home; there was a series of six messages, all from me, each sounding increasingly desperate. I phoned Mark's parents, Della and Tom; trying to sound casual, while really inside I didn't know whether to be angry or terrified. 'Have you heard from Mark today?'

'No.'

I quickly filled an awkward pause with an uncomfortable laugh, 'He must have gone out and not left a note ... perhaps he had a meeting he had forgotten to tell me about.' I needed to sound hopeful. I offered further excuses for the unexpected absence: 'Perhaps he had a job interview or an opening to follow.' I wanted them to believe the best. I promised to phone them when he came home.

Uncertain how things might work in the USA and not sure what to fear most, I called a friend, Sally, whose son is an attorney; I had reached a point where I was so fearful that I could easily believe that I was in trouble, too. I felt like the police might come for me; perhaps they would assume I knew what was going on. But what was going on? It was as if whatever Mark had done was highly contagious. Sally called her son, Paul, and he offered to speak to the inspector. They both assured me that Mark was not likely to be in jail.

Reacting to what we knew so far, Clare feared that Mark might come home soon. She had a sense that what might follow may not be good for the children or for me. And perhaps it was quite reasonable to suppose that the police might also return looking for Mark. We agreed that staying in a hotel for the night may be the best plan; that way, if he returned, Mark would not know where we were, only that we knew something was terribly wrong. A night's rest to calm down might be best for us all.

Clare and Kate made a game out of packing for Grace; as children do she packed enough to stay for a year. We gathered up overnight things for Joseph and a travel cot. Travelling for a one-night stay with a baby and a four-year-old is no light-weight affair! Grabbing the closest pen to hand, a pink felt tip, I left a desperate scribbled note in large rosy letters on the kitchen island:

Mark,
If you come home please call me on my cell phone –
I need to know you are safe
Alice

No customary love, no kisses.

CHAPTER 3

Hiatus of Time

Then like a cavalcade, we left the house. As we reached the top of our cul-de-sac there was a group of our neighbours standing at the corner. I noticed that they turned and stared at us. At the time I attributed it to the fact that we must have looked rather odd: a stream of cars leaving our house.

Clare drove my car. From the passenger seat, passing a highway of shops and restaurants, I observed that people were going out for dinner. I was struck by how their lives carried on as usual while mine seemed to be turning upside down and inside out. It made no sense to me. I wanted the world to stop.

We arrived at a hotel several miles from home. Clare checked us in and a concierge offered to help us up to our room. Although unable to engage in the usual pleasantries of such an exchange, I was exhausted and accepted the help. It was getting late as were secured at last in our temporary refuge. Joseph was crying and desperate for a quiet feed and

sleep. Grace sat next to me on the firm pull-out couch, as she
snacked on cereal bars and cheesy goldfish, watching Disney
television; formerly unknown midweek treats. After a
desperate attempt to nurse Joseph, perhaps the only comfort
at this time of terror, I laid him down in the unfamiliar travel
cot and thankfully, after some persuasion, he went to sleep.
Darkness began to fill the room.

I phoned Della and Tom back – they had heard nothing.
I tried to sound casual, 'A late meeting he has not told me
about, perhaps.' Della asked if we had argued: I wish!
I promised to call in the morning. I tried Mark's mobile again
but there was no answer. Clare had left, promising to return
for us first thing in the morning. In the grey light, Grace and
I tiptoed around the room getting her ready for bed.

On reflection, Grace must have been very confused and
frightened. It was exceptionally difficult to get her to bed. In
desperation, I relented to her sleeping in the same bed as me,
and fully clothed I lay down next to her while she settled;
somehow I needed to be close to her, too.

I felt very alone. In my head, I calculated the time in
England, Six hours ahead – 2 a.m.: how could I phone now?
But I so desperately wanted to speak to my mum. I sobbed
quietly, aching for the absence of my lost father. I needed him
so badly in that moment.

Lying there, I became aware that I was still damp from the
rain: my t-shirt clung to me, dank and sodden. Physical
awareness resumed: I felt cold and dirty. The sudden stillness
in the room was such a stark contrast from the race going on
in my head and the events of the previous hours.

I decided to risk a shower despite the potential noise. It

provided an oasis in which to cry more freely. As the water ran down my body I stood shaking, and wept with all of my heart.

Finally, I lay down next to Grace, her body provided warmth. But still I could not rest . . . 3 a.m. in England . . . 4 a.m. . . . perhaps I could call now? I desperately needed to hear my mum's voice in the darkness, something comforting and familiar. As I clock watched, the hours moved so painfully slowly. My mind ran wild over the events of the previous hours and imagined those to come. I bargained with myself: what would be a reasonable time to call? I finally relented. Waking my mum from her sleep, I poured out the little I knew: Mark was missing, a court order to search our home for child pornography and a business card for a postal inspector were the only clues; I could not piece together what was going on. Mum tried her best to calm me and took the telephone number of the hotel, promising to phone me back in the morning.

I closed my eyes, wishing sleep would come and provide respite. I could feel Grace breathing restlessly beside me, her twisting body nudging me off the edge of the bed. Exhausted, I climbed into the other bed and lay there still and silent, but my mind could not be held back from replaying the day's events.

I must have fallen asleep, if briefly. I know sleep did come because in that moment I had the most vivid dream. I saw in the darkness a long straight road; there were trees either side set back from the highway and the bright headlights of a black car emerged from the shadows. Then I woke with a start, knowing what I had seen to be real, and with a firm realisation that Mark was dead. A conversation came to mind: about six weeks earlier, as we sat in the late evening side by side on the sofa, Mark had told me we would be better off without him. He had said he could just drive into a tree. At the time I thought he was depressed; struggling with the idea that he could not support his family and desperate to release some of the daily stress he could see I was feeling. He was about to graduate with a master's degree but still felt diminished by my achievements and status as a university professor of medicine. Now, as I remembered this, I knew Mark would not be coming home. He had died on that road. The numbers on the clock continued to turn painfully slowly in the darkness. I could hear both of my children's gentle breathing and stirring. My heart ached.

It was 6.30 a.m. when a shrill page on my bleep from the university hospital rang out into the dark and silent hotel room. My baby and child had not yet stirred. Once again panic and adrenaline set in and paranoia gripped my every thought. I called back to the switchboard: 'Where are you, Dr Wells? Are you in the hospital?'

'Why?' I asked.

'I am not sure I can say . . .' replied the voice.

I thought, who's looking for me? How can I say I'm not at home? But then I answered, 'I am at a hotel,' and gave the details. 'Why do you want to know?

'Oh, Dr Wells, I'm not sure what to say. There is a man here looking for you . . . a state trooper. Stay where you are, they want to come and talk with you.' The kind stranger from the switchboard hung up the phone.

At once my mind was in a state of panic. I really believed in that moment that the police were coming for me. The earlier dream forgotten for now, I thought they had arrested Mark. That they thought I was involved. But involved in what? I did not know . . . Terrified thoughts filled my mind: they would take me from my children. I would be deported. I forgot that I was innocent.

The context for these irrational thoughts had been set a year earlier, during a flight home to England. I had sat next to a British woman who shared with me her distressing story. She had married an American, and they had had two children: this was a story not unlike my own. Her marriage was not a happy one. A cultural canyon existed between her and her husband. They were divorcing but the American family court had given the father full custody of the children. In her words: they did not want to lose their own citizens to an immigrant who would not stay. She had found she increasingly had no rights. The loss of her children had left her heartbroken. This story had often echoed in my thoughts when our own marriage hit troubled ground. When Mark and I argued he would tell me if I left our marriage he would keep the children. I was the 'legal alien' with minimal rights. In those threats I felt trapped with no choice but to stay. Now today, 26 July, I found myself waking up in my own nightmare, where nothing seemed an unlikely outcome.

I called Clare, 'they're coming here . . . for me. Clare, I don't know what to do . . . the state trooper is coming . . .' Clare was on her way. I was terrified.

By now, Joseph was awake and crying and Grace was saying she was hungry. The shrill sound of the hotel phone rang out loudly into the mayhem of the room: 'Mrs Wells, there is someone in reception for you.' I picked up Joseph; no one would separate me from my children. I began madly searching for my shoes as I called to Grace to come to me. We would go down to the lobby; perhaps it would be safer there. They could not come up to the room. But I could not find my shoes. Where are my shoes? I was in a state of panic.

Then there was a firm knock at the door. I opened the door to find a state trooper and a woman in a dark suit standing outside. Entering the room, they asked me to sit down. I held Joseph in my arms and Grace huddled next to me, on the hard, barely functional hotel sofa. We were overwhelmed by these two strangers towering above us.

'Mrs Wells, I am sorry to have to tell you your husband has been killed in a car accident. He died at the scene.'

A little voice reached through the fog: 'Mummy, where is Daddy?' 'Mummy I am hungry.'

It was as if I had been shot. I sat stunned. No time for the ricochet. Grace needed me. She was hungry. My husband was dead. Reality felt unreal. Uncertain how to meet the competing needs around me, I allowed the women, a stranger, in her black suit to take Grace downstairs to the breakfast buffet. Grace was hungry, she was focused on her immediate need; she seemed not to have heard what was being discussed, that Daddy was dead.

Joseph still in my arms, the officer stood before me and briefly explained the details: Mark had been involved in a collision with another vehicle seventy miles south of where we lived, at 8.30 p.m. the previous evening. He gave me the name of the officer who had attended the scene of the accident and suggested I call him for more detail when he returned to duty that afternoon. A trooper had been parked outside our house since last night, having had no reply at the door; they had anxiously awaited our return. In the early hours of the morning, a neighbour getting up for work had suggested they try the university hospital where I worked.

The trooper still towering above me rapidly excused himself and the lady in the black suit reappeared. She did not seem to know what to say except that Clare had arrived and was with Grace choosing breakfast. I have always assumed she was a bereavement officer, although she did not give me a card or number to call. Perhaps I appeared well supported already. They asked no questions and offered no follow-on support. It seemed that they knew nothing of the postal inspectorate search of our home. I was so stunned by the news of Mark's death, it didn't occur to me to ask. In the next moment the phone rang, and seemingly relieved to have reason to excuse themselves, they both left.

The call was from my mum. Having told her the news, she said she would talk to my brother and come as soon as she could. So many shadows had suddenly cast a veil over the world as we knew it. Clare phoned work to tell them Mark had died and let them know I would not be in. In that moment, I felt like the featureless wallpaper stuck to that hotel room wall. I remember nothing only that I had been stunned numb.

Reeling in the activity of packing up after a one-night hotel stay with two small children, and in a state of exhaustion, we gathered ourselves up and left the hotel.

Mark's mum called to say she was on her way and had I

heard from Mark. I replied, 'No.' I was trying to hold it all together for the children, who were circling my feet. I wonder what story she imagined for this yet unknown chain of events. My in-laws were very aware that our marriage was once again encountering troubled times and I know that I had often seemed alien to them. Mark was missing. Did they wonder what had happened between Mark and I this time; perhaps he had left me.

Standing in the hotel lobby, I became conscious of the conspicuous attention we had drawn from the morning events. I wanted to shrink away. But as Clare brought the car around, the atmosphere I felt was not one of curiosity and intrigue, but shock and tearful compassion; the hotel told us there would be no charge for the room. Out of sadness comes a great many small acts of kindness. The world for all its misery has many tiny pockets of compassion.

By now I was empty and my mind was overfull. Grace did not seem to have heard what the policeman had said or at least had not registered it. I would need to make a lot of phone calls, clarify what was happening and had happened, and somehow absorb all this myself, before I revisited telling Grace that her daddy had died. So as if by rote, I took both Grace and Joseph straight into nursery.

I hurried along the central corridor to Grace's classroom first and, after hugging Grace and hanging up her bag, I called her teacher out into the hall. I starkly told her that Grace had had a very difficult night and may be tired; that her father had died but I would prefer no one mentioned this or treated her any differently. My instincts told me that routine would be where Grace would find safety from the chaos of the previous twelve hours. I would come back in the early afternoon to collect her and then take her somewhere safe to explain her daddy's death.

In Joseph's nursery room, it was not unusual for parents to arrive worn down by a sleepless night and so a motherly teacher naively asked me if all was OK. 'Had we had a bad night? You look tired.'

'None of us had much sleep last night' I replied.

She put her arms around me and then it just slipped out: 'Joseph's daddy was killed in a car accident last night.' The nursery team enveloped me in their arms, unable to make sense of what they had heard. They were visibly shocked that I was there at all. I was trying to keep myself together; building a protective shield to save face. Having managed the drop off, I needed to get home.

In the brilliant blue sky and morning sun, Clare drove us back to the house. The familiar short journey felt so empty. There were a few fallen limbs of trees strewn about in the streets, but these were the only remaining physical sign of the fierce and destructive storm of the evening before. As we came over the brow of the hill, we could see two small figures on the path leading up to the front door. Jenny and Julie, close friends and colleagues from work, had left the hospital on hearing the news that Mark had died, determined to come and offer their support. Someone else would hold the fort on other people's despair today.

I climbed out of the car and collapsed in a heap into Jenny's arms. I could not hold back anymore. Right there on the sloping lawn of our home, I broke down in sobs and any remaining physical strength drained from me. At that moment, I felt a wave of acute loss come over me. All I could say was, 'I so need my dad.' He had always been my rock in times of crisis. As I fell to my knees, I needed him to hug his little girl and tell her he was here. I longed for his safe strong arms to lift me up just as they had done before when I was his little child.

Between them, Jenny, Clare and Julie got me inside. They held me until the acute shock compounded by arriving home subsided back into numbness and disbelief.

As we gathered ourselves to consider what we should do next with a hot drink, we discovered that I had no coffee in the house. The house had become a shell in recent months, frozen meals were an increasingly prominent necessity, and we had begun unconsciously to lack the comforts of a home: Starbucks providing the latte in the early mornings and at work. And so a shopping party was deployed to gather essentials for those who would gather around their newly-widowed friend.

It was not long before Mark's mum arrived: alone. Tom had gone to work, confident, I am sure, that this was just another marital 'tiff'. I had mustered some strength by now. As Della came in through the door into the bright open plan hallway, I said, 'You had better sit down.'

I think she must have guessed what I was about to say as the words fell from my lips. Sitting at the dining room table just a few steps from the front door, I said, 'Della, Mark died in a car accident last night.'

She broke in an instant, like a shattered glass, screaming, 'No not another one . . . not another son. It has to be a mistake.

No not Mark!' Mark was their son who had 'made good'. He had done well in their eyes and they were very proud of his achievements. Della's life had been shaken before by the traumatic death of a child. Mark's stepbrother, Rick, had been killed by his wife with a kitchen knife. It was in self-defence, and a challenging court case had ensued before eventually Della was reconciled with her granddaughter and daughter-in-law. The brutal death of another son brought Della to her knees.

I told her the sketchy outline of what I knew about the accident and held her as she wept; a brief moment of intimacy with the mother-in-law I scarcely knew or understood.

I called my father-in-law and regretfully told him the news on the phone, so I could be sure he would join us immediately. I didn't know how to comfort Della, nor did I have the strength. We needed him to come right then and there. A kind friend drove him to us and, in his own state of disbelief, Tom arrived just after lunch. Hours seemed suspended and heavy with expectation. Exhausted, I retreated upstairs to 'pump'. I was grateful for the excuse to avoid and escape conversation. I hoped to try and sleep before I returned to the task of telling Grace what had happened.

Sleep never came. Too much adrenaline permeated my veins. There were now too many anticipated 'to dos' and too many questions hanging in the air without answers.

I called the state troopers' office to find out when I could speak with Trooper Worth about the accident. I would have to wait a little longer. He would be in later that afternoon. His shift started at 3.30 p.m. I called Sally to see if Paul had been able to reach the postal inspector. He had not. I was caught in a waiting game. A little bit of me remained fearful that I might still be implicated in whatever it was that Mark had done. It did not occur to me that these many different branches of law enforcement and public safety would not communicate with each other and the postal inspector, Jack Hutton, did not know Mark had died. I lay down again but I did not sleep, I remained too anxious for answers.

At last 3.30 p.m. came: Trooper Worth had been on duty the night before; he had been called to an accident on the outskirts of a small town, between a Honda Accord and a Winnebago. The owners of a home set back from the road had heard a loud crashing noise on the perimeter of their property at about 8.36 p.m. The road markings suggested that Mark had crossed the central line of the road hitting the mobile home head-on. His car had then veered off the road and the van had rolled over and off onto the opposite bank. I was told Mark was killed on impact. The driver of the van was alert at the scene and airlifted by helicopter to the nearby hospital. His injuries were serious but not critical. Later, it struck me that he was the same age as Mark; from the accident report I could see just four days separated their birthdays.

The coroner certified Mark's death 21.12 at the scene of the crash; just as we had travelled to the hotel. While all about me strangers were going out to dinner and to the grocery store, business was as usual, Mark was transferred from this scene to the nearest funeral home. Trooper Worth observed that there was a half-empty beer can in Mark's car and another unopened can had rolled onto the floor from the rear seat. But he made no accusations. He expressed his concern for myself and gently asked me a few questions. I explained that I was

not sure where Mark had been that evening or why he had
been travelling south. Trying to rationalise his journey, I
explained that Mark sometimes had meetings out of town for
the graduate mentoring programme. Indeed, his mentor for
the MBA programme lived in that area. I was still desperate to
excuse or perhaps protect my husband from cause and effect.

The trooper gently asked if I had concerns about it being
any more than an accident. I said no. I desperately told him
that it was not like Mark to drink and drive, but inside I was
worried this was the case. The trooper had sent off a blood
alcohol level and would complete his report. He reassured me
he would be recording this as an 'accident' and I would receive
the death certificate from the coroner once all the
investigations were complete. There was no need for a post-
mortem. The impact of the crash was self-evident. Cause of
death: multi-blunt trauma. A death certificate: I had
completed so many of those in my professional life.

Finally, I was advised of the location of the car at the nearby
wrecker's yard so that I could retrieve its contents and inform
our insurance company. Trooper Worth asked me to contact
the funeral parlour as soon as possible so that they could
make arrangements to move Mark's body to nearer home. In
an effort to comfort me, our conversation ended with the
remark that he did not think Mark had suffered; I could call
him anytime if I had any more questions.

I had so many questions.

CHAPTER 4

Covered by the Dust

In the early days after my own father had died, Grace and I walked on the sparsely wooded trails just below our house. In a clearing was a little bridge with a shallow creek running below it. She remembered playing there with my dad, tossing stones into the water. We came to fondly name it 'The Daddy Bridge'. One Sunday afternoon together, Mark threw stones with Grace there, too. I decided we would go to this place that afternoon. It would be away from the house, quiet, and for us both had been a place of comfort where we remembered my dad. In my mind, I thought perhaps in time Grace might need a place to be with her dad, too. I collected Grace early from nursery, planning to return later for Joseph. Grace needed some space of her own.

We walked across the vast empty space of the arena-sized car park, just a short distance from the nursery, which leads into the back end of the creek. Holding her tiny hand, I explained to Grace I needed to talk to her and that was why we had left nursery early today.

It was a starkly hot day with no obvious place for respite from the sun. The humidity created steam as it hit the hot tarmac. I don't really remember the words or how we got there, but by the time we reached the bridge over to the creek I had told Grace her daddy had died. Grace clung to me, crying. 'No Mummy. Daddy isn't dead.'

Just then, as I looked around at our treasured space, I was struck by the appearance of the bridge: it had been vandalised and was ruined by litter and graffiti. There was no flowing water, the creek was dry and the ground cracked in the scorching sun. The grass and bushes were brittle and drained of all their colour. It was in a state of ruin. How pertinent and yet how devastating that our place of refuge should appear quite the opposite today. We did not linger, but briefly said what felt like an inadequate prayer and retreated home.

Our comprehensive palliative care team was fully equipped to help our patients and their families in their loss: a team of doctors, nurses, chaplain, art therapist, psychologists, music therapists and bereavement specialists. Ironically, I could not have been in a better position or more supported; skilled colleagues wanted to help and they did with all their might. And so remarkably: Julia, our art therapist from work, came that evening to play with Grace, encouraging her to paint. Together, they painted a beautiful colourful butterfly on the front of a sketch book Julia gave to Grace.

This canvas became a place for us to try and help Grace draw out her thoughts. It took time and a lot of patience, not just paints. In her short story in pictures, a boy wants to play with a beautiful happy butterfly. All is well until we turn the page. He catches the butterfly and traps it in a cage. There is then a dark shadow of a figure, who is painted in black in her picture; he stands between Grace and the butterfly that is tightly bound up in the cage. Turn the page, and the butterfly is set free and returns to her family. She is happy again.

There was little time to breathe in that first twenty-four hours. That afternoon, a stream of phone calls went on: reporting to the car insurance company, setting up an appointment with a local funeral home for the next day, calling the coroner's office and the funeral home where Mark was located. Never had he seemed so distant. Spin, spin, spin.

Later that day, I finally reached the postal inspector, Jack Hutton, heavy hearted with expectation. It had felt that this call might hold all the answers, as on the surface it seemed to be the start of it all. When I explained to him that Mark was dead he was palpably shocked. He asked for the state trooper's details so that he could confirm the details of Mark's death.

Reassuringly, both had promised they would be discreet; they had no need to disclose the content of their investigations. My fear was that our family would be the subject of the evening news. I feared that our story would reach local TV or newspapers or that the other victim of the accident might hear fragmented details of the life of the 'other man'. I was so fearful. What if the insurance company heard too and felt unable to compensate in these circumstances? But what were the circumstances? It remained just as unclear. All I knew was that I felt such shame.

Inspector Hutton explained that his investigation was ongoing; they were not yet clear about Mark's involvement in internet child pornography. This was the first time I'd heard the word 'child' spoken out loud, and it hung heavy in the air. He worked for the postal service inspectorate in the department investigating internet crimes against children. This team had been at our house yesterday with a SWAT team from the city police, following a period of weeks observing Mark's activities both under close surveillance and on the internet. They had half-expected Mark not to be home. Circling the house, a dozen bullet-proofed officers descended on Mark as he had casually answered the front door. The interview had lasted about six hours.

Inspector Hutton described how they had seen him leave as they pulled away in the late afternoon: about 5.30 p.m. Mark had left the house; my unheard distress calls remained on the answerphone. The inspector and his team had had no reason to suspect Mark was doing anything other than going to the grocery store, as he had told them he needed to do: to collect provisions for dinner. He had been calm and candid during the long interview and house search. He had cooperated fully, giving them passwords for email accounts and other details, while not implicating himself. They had removed all the computers, cameras and related equipment from the house. An investigation was underway; they did not yet have an arrest warrant.

There was one missing piece in the search: a post-office box key. Mark had first come to their attention because of packages being delivered to a box at our local post office. Did I know where the key might be? I didn't know there was a post-office box let alone where there might be a key. Inspector Hutton said if I should find it I should let him know.

We arranged to speak again and he agreed to meet me when

more information had been gathered from their investigation. The inspector would be my only path into the whole other life of a husband I was no longer certain I knew. He was taken aback by Mark's death. Following a moment of silence at the end of the call, perhaps needing time himself to reflect on what had happened, he said, 'I am very sorry, Mrs Wells.'

I sat alone, on the edge of the bed we had once shared.

There was a lot of coming and going that day from the house, and with each journey to and fro from nursery I felt the glare of our neighbours upon us. Our location at the bottom of a cul-de-sac made me feel like I was in a tiny goldfish bowl and that our only exit was under the full watch of those surrounding us. Had the same neighbours watched the incredulous events of the previous afternoon unfold before their eyes?

My refuge that day came from nursing baby Joseph upstairs in the quiet of my bedroom. As I held my little son he was balm for my soul once again, just as he had been ten months earlier, fluttering inside me when he was no more than a bump, when Dad had died.

This moment of intimacy was shattered by a neighbour, who burst into the bedroom with a cream pie under the pretence of, 'Oh Alice is there anything I can do, we are all so shocked . . .' Clare and Kate were hot on her heels from downstairs, as she had let herself in, and they swiftly asked her to leave. I was fuming, and remain just as convinced today of her motivation and role as neighbourhood gossip; she had come in for some hot off the press news, the inside scoop from the widow herself. I allow myself this one little slice of bitterness.

When calmer, I wrote a measured response to the outflow
of attention from neighbours and people at nursery; a brief
note, which a friend kindly delivered to all of our neighbours
the next day. It simply stated that we needed space, time and
would approach them rather than the other way around if we
needed anything. I felt very protective of the children and
dreaded the rumour and speculation. I didn't want chatter to
occur in Grace's earshot. I was sure that there was mixed
motives for this unwanted attention: concern, of course, but
also speculation, sensationalism. And I felt strongly that what
the children needed was routine and to be treated as normal
– not drama.

07/27/07

Dear Friends

*As most of you know I lost my husband in an automobile
accident earlier this week. I have been truly amazed at the
outpouring of love and support from my family and friends. I so
appreciate all of your offers to help and am comforted in knowing
that I can depend on all of you when the time comes that I will
need help. Please know that I will contact you once we have
established some sort of routine and needs arise.*

*As Grace needs the comfort and familiarity of her routine, she
will be returning to school next week. I know that being with her
friends and being treated normally as she is welcomed back will
help her through this difficult time. Thank you for all of your love
and concern for our children.*

Much love, Alice Wells

As the day unfolded, some of the detail began to fill in, but there remained a lot of uncertainty and unknowns. In the early evening, my mum called and my brother. I told them everything I knew. They tried hard to temper my desperate conclusions from the little I knew. I remember feeling so far away from them and so desperate to have my brother take the reins; just as my dad would have done had he been alive. But although I really wanted my brother to say 'I'm coming on the next flight', he didn't. He couldn't; he had commitments and a family of his own to support through the impact Mark's death and the Postal Inspection Service investigation had on them. Mum had booked her flight and was leaving Saturday morning. My longest and most faithful friend happened to call in the midst of all that was going on. Why she called then I do not know; another blessing. She offered to come over and I think if the funeral had not been just three days away, she would have been there. She phoned me regularly in the weeks that followed and when I finally came home to England, she was waiting to help me through all the changes. I was blessed by so many good friends.

The sun finally went down on that long day and people retreated to their own spaces. As I stood at the sink, washing up baby bottles, the children asleep at last in their beds, I saw my tearful reflection in the kitchen window. Lost for a moment, I felt the warmth of Mark's strong arms wrap around me, his cool breath on my neck, transporting me to another time. For one intimate moment, I believed he was there and all would be well.

As the light dwindled and silence descended on the house, I ventured downstairs for the first time, to the basement and Mark's office. Our house had been built into a hill and the basement backed onto the lower ground garage and the back deck. It had little natural light but the guest bedroom and office provided a cool refuge in the heat of the summers. I stepped over the wires that were strewn across the floor of Mark's office; determined to look for evidence of what had happened and perhaps find the post-office box key that Inspector Hutton had spoken about. I was desperate to seek out clues, to understand what had happened and had been happening: to piece together my husband's life. He had increasingly felt like a stranger in the last twenty-four hours.

Even in the best part of the day, the basement office was a stale and lightless place. There were no windows and now more than ever it seemed dank and airless. This place provided perfect refuge from a tornado, but little else.

First my eyes were drawn to some Post-it Notes with names and telephone numbers on Mark's desk, written in his familiar hand and in technical pencil. He did not like to use a pen, he had once told me: too permanent and he might make a mistake. What does this say about the man and his actions: fearful of leaving an indelible stain? And then, seemingly quite deliberately, a receipt fell to the floor from the papers on his desk detailing a debit to the post office: for the box. The ease with which I found evidence of the post-office box perhaps points to a chaotic and careless police search. The name registered for the box had been subtly changed: 'Mr Mike Wall'. I did not find a key, only proof that the box existed.

My gaze now was drawn to the contents of the cupboards and dresser drawers, which lay scattered on the floor among the array of computer cables and paper: bank and credit card statements. Scanning for more information, the credit card balances shook me, as did their detail. There were multiple transactions for foreign money transfers and payees I did not recognise, leading to an outstanding balance of over $15,000. I sat on the floor weeping tears of disbelief at the secret life my husband had led. How will I ever pay these debts? Who was this man I had lived with for nearly ten years? How far did his secrets go?

STEP ONE The Elephant Enters the Room

I don't know how she got there. I had planned to lie down to rest in the darkened room; hoping for peace. She had crept in; her presence was incongruous.

Once the elephant arrived I could not escape her presence. She squeezed me to the edges of my refuge. I hid beneath the covers, but as I did so I felt her weight cause our marital bed to sink. She pulled at the covers; as they twisted in her might any warmth drifted away.

Fear descended. My ear tuned into her breathing. Elephants take just five breaths per minute at rest. I found myself falling in step, soon having to come up for air.

In the silence of the night, my heart and hers beat a tune; a shifting rhythm formed as I took two or three beats for her every one, this duet resounding against my eardrum.

She was formidable; I turned to face her. Our eyes met at last in the dim light; warm brown eyes beneath their wiry lashes drew me in. They were kind and knowing; full of regret. Her head lowered, tears fell, running down her coarse elephant cheeks onto the crisp white sheets below.

But I should not have been deceived; better had I prepared for the wild fervour that was only moments away from this unnerving stillness. She shook and, as she did so, released the shrill gut-wrenching yell of a lost mother calling desperately for her young.

CHAPTER 5

Gathering

Friday 27 and Saturday 28 July

The next morning, Clare took the children to nursery having stayed the night with us. I prepared to go with Della and Tom to the local funeral home where Mark's body had been transferred.

In those early days, I began avoiding conversations with my mother-in-law that might lead us to questions about what had happened the night Mark had died. I kept the truth limited to the facts of the accident. The rationale I clung to then was that they were elderly and I needed to protect them from the horror that was unfolding. I did not want to be the destroyer of their image of their son.

Kate, having organised her own mum's funeral just four months earlier, offered to go with us to the funeral office. I was so grateful for her support. I had never organised a funeral in America before, although I had attended several and was very aware they were different to back home.

No one doubted my ability to drive that morning until I backed right into the side of Kate's SUV on the drive. My head was on my shoulders but my mind was somewhere else. Kate drove us instead, while I apologised profusely for the large dent in her car. I suspect she hadn't the heart to make a fuss about it to her newly-widowed friend whose life was falling apart around her.

A strange calm came over me as we sat at a long boardroom table in the funeral home, completing paperwork and plans for Mark's funeral. Tom waited outside in the car park, unable to come inside. Della became tearful and stepped outside into the hall; Kate went out to comfort her. I declined an embalming and viewing. Instead, I requested he be cremated before a memorial service that Sunday afternoon. In retrospect, it all happened very quickly, but at the time it seemed for the best. Under the guidance of the funeral director, we wrote a small piece for that evening's and the next day's newspaper, in case there were college friends or tutors who might want to attend; a small memorial that spoke of what a dedicated father Mark had been.

The funeral director then went off to locate Mark's valuables. On returning he expressed concern that they could not find Mark's wedding ring, but handed me Mark's wallet and watch. As they passed them into my hand I felt connected again to a husband who had just died. It had not occurred to me to take the seventy-mile journey south to see his body, or to confirm it really was him. I had all the stark truth I needed to believe it was Mark. Sometimes I regret not taking an opportunity to see him, to say 'goodbye'. But then, I wonder what he would have looked like. I have pondered if they discreetly hoped I would say no to a viewing. He must have been terribly wounded; crumpled like his car. I am not sure how I now remember him, but perhaps it was best I didn't see him again, just then.

I have seen many dead bodies in my role as a doctor looking after the dying patient; it does not disturb me but it does feel a mixture of intimate and solid cold. I think my uncertainty of how I felt about Mark in that moment had a part to play. If I spent a few intimate moments with his body then what would I say in the creeping silence to the man I loved who now was unrecognisable in ways beyond the flesh?

Other questions hang in the air of that boardroom moment: did he cast off his wedding ring that night? Was he struck by how 'over' our marriage and our life might be? The ring wasn't special really. Ironically, he had found it discarded in a car park, and when we married we were not flush with cash so we were happy with the find.

Della returned to the room with Tom, and I suggested that she should keep Mark's ashes, and chose something to put them in. In that moment, it seemed right that he return to his parents. I felt disconnected from the man I had joined in marriage. I no longer knew what or how to feel about the man I had loved. I did not want him near. Della spent some time with Tom deciding on a precious box for the ashes, as she did so I looked at the car keys and wallet in my hand for the first time. I noticed a faint smear of blood in the deepest crevice of the key: Mark's blood, a very real reminder of his life and his death. These few personal effects were so little to hold on to.

I parted from my in-laws in the car park of the funeral home; they were to return to their home in the neighbouring

state, gathering extended family for the upcoming funeral.
I returned home with Kate and began more phone calls. There
were more distressing calls that day: the first a return call to
the car insurance company adjuster who had called asking for
the details of the accident. He advised me that the driver of
the other vehicle had been airlifted to hospital and his
insurance company had advised them he was in a critical
condition. The insurance adjuster challenged me: could my
husband have intended to cause an accident? Had he been
drinking? And then he sowed a seed of threat: if the claim of
the other party exceeded our policy limit, I would be liable for
their costs, which seemed to him likely if the other driver was
as ill as current information suggested. He would visit him in
hospital and let me know.

I put the phone down and collapsed. Could things get any
worse? Mark was dead, the circumstances terrifying. Mark
had died leaving thousands of dollars in credit card debt and I
might also be liable for hundreds of thousands of dollars in
damage liability. The adjuster was just doing his job,
minimising the losses for the insurance company. The payout
would be huge. In his efficiency, he failed to grasp the human
loss in this matter: a husband and father had died.

Clare was furious at my obvious distress and called them
back to complain. Immediately they recognised their error,
and we were connected with a more sympathetic department,
dedicated to cases of fatalities and loss. They were to handle
our case from now on. The disgruntled adjuster also called
briefly to apologise for his abruptness, yet still keen to have
the last word, he closed his call by maintaining that if there
was alcohol or suicide in question, the company would not be

obliged to cover the losses.

Distressed by the thought that Mark had caused considerable harm to the stranger in the other vehicle, I called the trooper again to verify how the other driver was doing. I felt some responsibility for this other man, whose date of birth was so close to Mark's. Trooper Worth dismissed the notion that the other driver was in anyway critical. He had been airlifted because of the rural location not because of his condition. The trooper expressed his concerns for us and explained he had sent a blood alcohol level but did not expect it to be high; the majority of the beer was sloshed into the foot wells of the car, not consumed. It would be about two weeks for the result. He saw no reason for any further investigation. I remember, he asked if I thought it could be suicide and I told him that although there was little doubt Mark had been distressed at the time of the accident, I also had no doubt he would not wish to risk another man's life. If it had been suicide he would have found a good tree or wall, not another vehicle. I convinced myself in that moment as well, and still want to believe this version of the truth.

Clare is an amazing organiser and by this point had been out and bought a notebook for us to record telephone numbers and essential information. She helped me call and enlist the help of friends and colleagues as we pulled together the memorial service. I don't think my friends dared leave me alone for long in those first days; they could not bear the thought of it. I existed and my balm was the children whose daily needs continued unchanged.

My counsellor and friend Faye came to see me, but I remember little of what we talked of in this and the weekly sessions that followed: surely the story of the events, the thoughts of the previous twenty-four hours, the challenging conversation with the car insurance company and how best to carry on. I would learn first-hand how telling a trauma story over and over untangles it, distances it from the self. But there is a catch: the body remembers in the very fabric of your being and in fine detail how it felt and how to express distress in very physical ways, and so the trauma can re-emerge like an assassin and catch you out. Faye had held concerns about Mark close to herself since first meeting him for a 'married couples' session, just before my father had died. Nevertheless, she like others was shocked at the events that had ensued. Together with Clare, she offered to go down to the accident site and to retrieve items from Mark's car the next day. Even if I had felt able to go, I don't think they would have let me, but someone needed to go soon to the car. We needed to look for the post-office box key.

On Saturday, God sent his army: friends came to look after both of the children, clean my house ready for a reception after the memorial service, flowers arrived, cards began to flood in and Clare and Faye departed to see the wrecked car, an hour's drive away. Amid the ebb and flow, Marvin, our hospital chaplain, came to comfort me. Marvin is a gentle giant, an African American with a voice that is like velvet kisses and sturdy hands fit to entrust and cup your deepest needs. In what felt like a surreal fog, we planned Mark's service music, the military banners and salute, Marvin's dedication and the readings. I decided I would do a final dedication myself; Mark was a loner and didn't have close friends. Before he left, Marvin prayed with me, and this felt like a brief moment of respite.

The wave of activity returned: food arrived for the following day and Julia came to paint with Grace in her book. Clare arrived back from the trip to the wrecker's yard, disturbed by all she had seen that day. She explained that she and Faye had seen the accident site and spoken to the neighbours who had responded to the accident. Faye had taken some photos; Clare would get them developed and hold on to them until I wanted to see them. It would take me some time.

In the crumpled front of the car, which had to be opened with a crowbar, Clare and Faye had found the post-office box key in the shattered glove box. In the strangely preserved trunk of the car was a jacket and a child's blanket; Faye had taken this home to wash: 'it was dirty'. She and Clare both assumed the blanket belonged to Grace and might be treasured. When it was returned to me freshly laundered, I had never seen it before and I tossed it away as something too closely associated with Mark's final hours. Only later, after I had thrown it away, did I realise that perhaps this might have been valuable evidence. There were few other personal effects in the car – an old baseball cap, a single worn out tennis shoe and an old sheet. The car itself was a mess.

John, a good friend who is also English, and had met my parents several times on their visits, collected Mum from the airport. Mum was relieved to see us and be with us. It must have been so hard for her in that waiting time before she arrived. Grace was thrilled to see her. Friends left to give us some time alone and I remember little more than that we cried.

CHAPTER 6

Sunday Funeral Blues

Sunday arrived hot and sunny. Grace and I had talked about the funeral and she decided she would rather stay at home with Julia, who had offered to come and be with her at home or at the service. I think I was quite relieved that she wanted to stay at home to paint and play. Joseph's nursery teacher was coming at lunchtime to look after him, a lovely motherly lady who had only our needs at heart. I spent the morning looking after Joseph and preparing my dedication to Mark. Our closest neighbour took Grace to church to the morning service with her children, friends that Grace was used to playing with.

For the purposes of the day, and I suppose at that time for my own sanity, I had convinced myself by now that Mark's death had been a tragic accident and the allegations of child pornography perhaps meant he had looked at teenagers on the internet and had owned some images of them. He had been quite upfront at times about his attraction to the young girls in scanty bikinis in an Australian advert, or to the reality programme searching for the next 'Cheetah Girl'. He liked teenage girls physically: nothing more than this. Of course, there is nothing OK about this, but at this time I was desperate, clutching at what felt like the least horrifying crime that could fall within the definition. My denial helped me to believe my eulogy and feel closer to him on a day marking his death.

At the funeral home, I remember feeling numb but somehow also aware that beneath the surface stirred a very restless feeling. I began to recite the words of Psalm 46: 'God is our refuge and strength, an ever-present help in trouble . . .' I felt terrified by the idea of being out in public, that all eyes might be on us, and uncertain how I would withstand the service and speaking. I remember sitting in a little room just off the chapel as people arrived, with Kate holding my nervous hand. I sat and prayed. I held in my mind's eye an image of God holding me in his hands. I thought of my own father and how he would fold me into his arms when I cried and give me the certainty I could go on.

My mum volunteered to greet people at the door in my absence. She must have been daunted as she hardly knew any of these people. I came in just as everyone was seated, gripping onto my mum and Kate's hands. Separating me from the front pew was a walk down a very different aisle from the one I had happily floated down nine years earlier in my father's hands. Marvin gave me a warm nod to let me know he was there.

There was no coffin, just a few flowers, a photo of Mark which Della had chosen and a double picture frame of the children. On an overhead screen we played a photo album

Mark had created a few weeks earlier of the children, he had entitled it 'Our Little Angels' and it played to the song I felt the need to concentrate on: 'Grateful' by Art Garfunkel. This song reminds us of all we have; I needed to hold on to that thought and thought others might be comforted by it, too. The song came to an end and Marvin opened the service. I concentrated on the wood floor in front of me, aware that the room was full to the brim and conscious of eyes upon me.

There was no singing from the congregation; Mark had always felt uncomfortable in that part of a church service. He was unsure how to 'worship' in song. Instead, I had selected another recorded song, 'Sand and Water' by Beth Nielson Chapman, which she had written after her husband died leaving her with her young son. It is a song of hope, of meeting again. I intended it to connect people and, for that matter, my own mind with the children and all they had lost. I felt a sudden impulse to have my children in my arms and in a moment of crazy abandon got up, picked up the photo frame and returned to my seat clutching them. I wondered if people thought for an instant I was going crazy, but in that moment I did not care.

The honour guards came in and folded the United States flag, the Stars and Stripes, as part of military honours. They then handed the carefully folded flag to me as Mark's widow. It seemed odd, with all that I knew, to bestow this honour. But at that time only a few of us knew even just a part of the truth. The majority at the funeral, Mark's family and my work colleagues for the most part, believed he was a hero; he had served his country, and he was a loving father and husband who had been tragically lost.

Next, and by God's grace, I stood to give a dedication to Mark from the lectern. I was able to stand and look out at all those faces, hoping to recreate a glimpse into our life as I had known it and the man I had loved; to create a picture of the man who had brought me to this foreign land. I was strangely calm and in that moment believed all that I said. Doubt did not cast its turn about me, nor did I let my mind wonder if my neighbours, who stood at the back, might question the legitimacy of all I had said. I looked along the pews at Mark's brother, Jack, and his parents crumpled with their grief; his uncle, aunt and cousins still reeling from their own grief for a son who had died the previous summer.

And this is what I said:

'Be still, and know that I am God' **Psalm 46**

'When I was lying awake in the early hours of Friday morning this verse came to me. Just forty-eight hours after Mark had died, I felt God speak to me. He told me I would speak here today and that I didn't need to be strong because he would be my strength. I perhaps should have prayed then for volume and I can't guarantee I won't need a Kleenex!

'I am a hopeless romantic. The story of how Mark and I met is a romantic tale that he loved to recount to people we met. I was an intern in England who spontaneously booked a trip to Egypt on my own. He was a staff sergeant in the United States air force on a tour of duty in England. Independently, we both booked our vacations to somewhere that intrigued us, at the last minute. We met on a tour from Cairo, where we both were staying, to Alexandria, one of the Wonders of the World. The tour bus stopped in the middle of the desert at a roadside pit stop. I came out of the bathrooms and Mark called over to me – he whispered in my ear, 'That large Egyptian man is blowing kisses to me – what should I do?' I spontaneously hugged Mark so that the large Egyptian would think we were together – and, as they say, 'the rest is history'. We would have been married nine years next month.

'Mark was a quiet man, quite uncomfortable in a crowd. I fell in love with his wonderfully silly sense of humour and later his wonderful way with our children. He was a marvellous father. When I came here eight years ago, Mark was my rock in a very hard transition, and when last year I told him my dad was dying from cancer, he held me safe.

'Mark was a perfectionist. He only ever wrote in technical pencil so he could correct himself. In his time in the air force, he was the 'go to' person in his team, and he also assumed that role in undergraduate and graduate school. He had a generous spirit. He loved to help others; giving money, when others turned away, to the man at the street corner who had run out of gas or helping fellow students with their projects before he finished his own.

'Mark's life was truly fulfilled by his children – especially Grace, who he adored. Mark became a very adept father taking her to Chuck E. Cheese's, the zoo and the science center. I loved to listen to them chuckle as he read Grace her bedtime story. Mark was happier behind the camera and so his recent gift to me was the musical slideshow of 'our little angels' you have just seen.

I would like to end with a poem. When we first met I would read poetry to Mark and so it seems a fitting way to say goodbye now. I just would like to add how blessed we are as a family to have family and friends to lean on and help us through this – thank you to you all . . .

And so I read 'Funeral Blues' – 'Stop all the clocks... For nothing now can come to any good.' – by W.H. Auden.

I found my way back to my seat and my mum gave my hand a squeeze. A prayer followed and then a departing song: Louis Armstrong's 'What a Wonderful World' – the opening song we had danced to at our wedding with such hope and expectation. I stood, legs not my own, to walk to the exit. I was struck by how many friends and colleagues had come to support me. They did not know Mark but had come to his funeral. Other than his family, parents from the day care and our neighbours, Mark had no friends attend. I spoke in a fog to those eager to express their regret and offer support. We then made our journey back to the house.

Walking into my house, it did not feel like my own; it was full of people. A loving army of friends had prepared a vast amount of food and were seamlessly attending to 'my guests'. I never had to ask. I found Grace and Joseph and Julia. It had not been an easy time for Grace and Julia. After we had left for the funeral service, Grace had spun into a full-blown tantrum and would not come out of the bathroom. She had wanted Mummy and to come to the funeral. Julia had struggled to comfort her in her distress and, for the first time since Thursday, Grace had been distraught. But now, with other children around, she was happy again. My advice to others about children and funerals has always been to let the children guide you in the decision, and to be aware of your own emotional limitations. I had not expected Grace to change her mind.

I remember very little of the rest of that afternoon except a blur of polite conversation, superficial explanation and the steady stream of condolences. I was exhausted, and although my body was present I'm not sure I was really there.

There were close friends who had been away and returned to the shocking news, desperate to piece together what had happened. I was aware that among all that were gathered there in our house some knew more than others, and some might have made assumptions or begun to spin out their own story in their heads, with their own anxieties. I felt neighbours were gossiping about us and felt very angry with them. It did not occur to me they might want to support me and the children, or be grieving themselves. I needed somewhere for my anger to go at that point and I was not ready to be angry with Mark. As I look back, I feel sad that I was not more generous in spirit to them.

Mark's family departed; his brother and father promised to return later that week to complete the office 'French door project' Mark had begun twelve months earlier, a labour of love for them. At last the house was quiet, friends had swept through and, apart from the vast quantities of food in the fridge, the house was restored to 'normal'.

Mum and I settled the children to bed, both of us exhausted. Mum, who was jet lagged and I suspect emotionally drained too, soon retired to bed. I went upstairs, but sleep evaded me. I felt like I was freefalling at speed down a terrifying deep, dark hole; and just like Alice in Wonderland, it felt surreal. I moved rooms but it didn't help. Soft pillows and cool sheets brought no respite. I was physically and emotionally exhausted, and yet every time I shut my eyes, my mind vividly ran events and anxieties through my head. I felt disconnected from me and did not know what to do with myself. As I tumbled into what seemed like an abyss there were no boltholes; I could find nothing to grab hold of which would have tempered the descent.

By the time Mum and Clare had taken the children into nursery the next morning I was in a terrible state. I had not slept, my emotions had reached fever pitch and the floodgates had opened; I could not stop crying. I had stopped thinking but tears just flooded out. Then my body began to shake. All of my senses felt alert and yet I was numb; unable to express verbally the horror of what had unfolded over the last few days. I had physically gone into shock. Every physical nerve fibre was firing like an electric storm. My teeth chattered, my body shook and I wanted to tear my body apart. I felt dirty. I ached for the man I loved, the man I thought I knew. I could find no peace.

In desperation, I took a small dose of the relaxant my doctor colleagues had brought to me in abundance the day after Mark died; until now their medical solutions had remained untouched in the kitchen cupboard. Yet relaxing was not an option, the medication only seemed to make things worse. I shook some more; my mum held me and tried her best to comfort me, but there was no comfort to be had. I had suddenly emerged from the fog; the enormity of what had happened and the permanence of the nightmare was upon me. I cried all day until I can only assume I was completely spent. The bereaved sometimes fear that if they start crying they will never stop and therefore a logical consequence might be that, like Alice in Wonderland they might drown in tears; somehow this does not happen. I am living proof. Like Alice, I had just floated downstream.

I spoke with Faye and arranged to see her at her office the next day. I became aware I needed help and I had no choice but to get it together: Grace and Joseph needed me. I could afford one so-called 'duvet day' but I could not retreat under the covers of my bed, escaping from the world and all its onlookers, and not come out. Life had to carry on and I had to be a part of it. There was so much that I had to tackle: paperwork, bills, finances, children and work.

It did not feel right to have friends prescribing medication or managing my self-destruction. But my situation was complicated by the idiosyncrasies that are the American health-care system. In the previous months, my own doctor had gone on maternity leave and I had not been able to find another doctor covered by my insurance who was taking new patients. Once again, Clare came to my rescue and booked an emergency appointment with an internist close by. The next morning, I visited him and he listened and prescribed me antidepressants to get me through the trauma. Right then, I had to decide to stop breastfeeding Joseph. It had been a source of comfort but I knew I could no longer physically give him all he needed. So I began to wean him and let others feed him when I could not. It was another difficult loss.

That Monday afternoon, I went with Mum to collect the children from day care. As we emerged from the car, the dad of Grace's closest friend approached me in the car park. Mum was just a few steps behind me. He did not hold back, asking, without a hint of caution, if his daughter had ever been left alone in my house with Mark. He was flustered and towered above me. I was floored and nearly passed out at his words. He had already made a leap that I had not: Mark had abused little girls. And a further leap: that Mark was capable of abusing his own daughter and her friends. 'No,' I replied. 'He was never alone with Jemma.'

I moved on and Mum grabbed my arm before I crumpled. Thank God she was there to hold me firm. What rumours were already circulating about Mark and what did people already know? If this man thought nothing of saying these things to me, what were other parents and the teachers saying to one another? What if Grace was to overhear them talking about her dad? I needed to protect my children.

I avoided eye contact with anyone and rushed through reception to collect Joseph. It was a place of relative safety and anonymity, as it seemed the parents in the baby nursery knew nothing of our loss, and the teachers were comforting. Mum gathered up Grace and we returned to the car.

Clare took control of the gossip mill at the nursery we both used. She called the director and requested that the chatter be stopped, that a letter be sent home with parents to clarify the need to be compassionate to the needs of Grace and Joseph and avoid rumour and gossip which could harm them as they grieved for their father.

CHAPTER 7

Counting Wednesdays

A week had passed and I moved psychologically from counting days to counting past the weeks. I was conscious of every Wednesday that passed in those first weeks. It heralded a milestone and another week since we had been more 'ordinary' and life did not defy expectation. It was as if I believed that the further I was from the 'day things changed' the less likely it was that we could go back to it and change what had happened; and the more real it had become. Eventually, the counting point became months and still each 25th of the month would feel different. The process of moving through the 25th each month continued for over a year.

That first Wednesday was incredulous. Only a week earlier, I had climbed out of bed with my usual frustrations about Mark and the hurried day ahead. I was blissfully unaware of his activities in our basement. He had seemed distant, but I had put this down to his lack of a job, the difficulties of the previous year: my father's illness, my time in England and Mark's own diagnosis of a haemorrhaging spinal cord tumour. I still had some hope that things would change for the better. Since my father's death, I had felt increasingly torn between living in the USA and 'home', England and my family. In recent months, this had started to become a reality. We had been looking at temporary apartments to rent to bridge us for a big move. Just two weeks before, we had been given a reasonable offer on the house and had received a privately drawn-up contract of sale to consider and sign by a developer who wanted to move his family to our area.

Now, a week on from Mark's death, and as it became apparent that we were the subject of florid neighbourhood gossip, I became anxious to contact the buyer and seek assurance that the sale would go ahead. It seemed a blessing that I had this opportunity in hand. The need to sell had taken on a new urgency; now I had no doubt about the need to move.

The buyer appeared to be avoiding my calls at first. When I finally cornered him, he told me his wife had changed her mind about moving. I crumpled at the news that our house was no longer sold. For a brief time this had been the silver lining: at least I had already sold the house. I could move as soon as we were ready, back to England without delay. Surely, I deserved some good luck!

Just a few weeks later, I discovered they had moved into another house a few blocks away. I was so mad at this man. I felt sure it was because he had heard the rumours of what had happened in our house; that he did not want to bring his family to a house where 'such goings on' occurred. I became anxious that my house would never sell if other buyers were to hear about Mark. Who would want to live here? My home felt tainted. And now I had to find another buyer for the house in an already difficult market. I was stuck in my 'goldfish bowl' for an indeterminate time.

It had always been hard living in a foreign country and now I felt very lost in the process of what to do when your husband dies, and how to go about processing his estate. Death by road accident did not have a 'how to booklet'. It seemed doubly difficult because I was not American; I don't know why I thought this because I had never had to do this in England either. I consider myself fortunate, though, as I had lots of knowledgeable friends and colleagues who helped me to navigate the system, otherwise I might have been truly lost. To register the death of a loved one I'd had to call a central automated telephone line and book an appointment at the local social security and benefits office. The process was very impersonal and frustrating, not at all compassionate: 'Press 1 for . . .' I soon discovered I could not do anything until I had the death certificate, and I was waiting for the coroner to issue this. I'd called to see when I might receive it: the next day, Wednesday 1 August. How many copies would I like? I wasn't really sure. I'd had no idea. My appointment with the social security was eventually booked for the following week.

I had become accustomed over the previous days of planning my trip to the mailbox at the end of our front path at a time when my neighbours were not out in the street, then I would not chance any conversations. Never had I received so much mail; even birthdays had never been marked by so many cards or flowers. I had not fathomed just how many designs of 'sorry for the loss of your husband' cards there might be

available. I think I exhausted the range. It really was quite
overwhelming. Cards flooded in daily, sometimes a dozen at a
time. There were condolences from friends far and wide, family
and university lecturers who had taught Mark. Some were
generous testimonials to Mark's character. Some were from
strangers to me: Mark's university tutors: 'During the several
years I knew him I gained an appreciation of his abilities and he
spoke so fondly of you and the children.' One in particular from
Mark's neurosurgeon stays with me: 'To me, he was the essence
of what is wonderful about the human spirit. He was intelligent
but with humility. His focus was on others not himself. Even
with an illness he kept his sense of humour and handled his
predicament with great dignity.' Their words made me cry;
perhaps that was good. Later, a sense of culpable duplicity would
creep over me: I was an accomplice in deception.

The death certificates (all ten of them, as advised) and the
accident report arrived on that same Wednesday morning.
Alone, I retreated into my office to read them. It was with
relief that I read the conclusion: Mark's death was accidental.
I wanted to hold on to the idea that he had not committed
suicide. I could not say the word; I could not believe he would
stoop so low as to endanger another person's life to meet his
own end. To this day I don't know for certain; he was
desperate, distraught and perhaps unaware of what he was
doing. He could have spun so easily out of control to cause
an accident.

I don't know why I had dreaded that the accident report
would mention why he was in turmoil: it is a legal report. It
doesn't deal with emotions but facts. Fact: Mark's car crossed
the meridian and hit a Winnebago driving the opposite

direction head on. Fact: He died at 8.36 p.m. and the coroner confirmed death at 9 p.m. Fact: He died from multi-blunt trauma. Relief, the insurance will be valid, both car and life insurance companies will be obliged to pay out. We would not face financial ruin on their account.

Despite this I did not feel reassured. There was no sense of peace. I did not feel financially secure. I still had no idea how much debt Mark had left. I only knew he was spending indiscriminately on pornography. I had no knowledge or understanding of how the world of internet pornography worked or how it was financed. Would there be more to come to light there? And still, there were four years of Mark's student loans to pay. At my lowest ebb I could only believe that there was more horror to come. I thought, only when I see the financial settlement for the car and house will I believe it will be OK.

A friend came to the house that afternoon to help me look through the 'stuff' in Mark's office and the basement. We were looking for clues to guide us and the postal inspector, in readiness for our meeting. We went through the remaining computer disks, DVDs and videos and any material that appeared related. In the mess, we found another camera the police had missed: our old digital camera. We put a box of evidence together, including the key to the post-office box.

I called Inspector Hutton to let him know we had found the key and a receipt for 'Mike Wall' for the post-office box. We agreed, I would drop off the key at their local office and then meet in person in two weeks' time, when he had had more time to gather together information for me. He was a busy man, away and working in other states over a large geographical area. How horrid it was to think that this man and his team were 'busy'.

By now, I was desperate to know if my children had been involved. Inspector Hutton assured me that there was nothing to suggest this. I explained my conversations at the day care, the concerns of others and my fear of this horror reaching the news media. He assured me that both he and the trooper at the accident would not disclose information. He thought it was most likely that the local police had been indiscreet when chatting with neighbours during the raid. He apologised, but the damage was done.

I remained quite terrified that no one would believe my innocence in Mark's actions. I still had fears that a police officer would come and take me; or that there would be legal action against us in Mark's name. As a 'legal alien' I feared for my rights; I was not a citizen. Because all that had happened so far was real, it did not seem unreasonable to have such thoughts. I could convince myself that I would be carted off as a co-child abuser/perpetrator and my children would be taken from me into care. I was catastrophising; but the world had started to tumble down around me in reality, so absurd extremes made sense.

Later that day, at my friend Sally's request, her attorney son, Paul, and his junior colleague, Greg, came to the house to go over the detail of what we knew and how to proceed. Pragmatically, they assured me of my innocence and that I was in no danger. I gratefully accepted their offer to go with me to meet the postal inspector, until we knew more about what Mark was accused of and where that might lead.

I spent the next two weeks waiting to meet the inspector imagining and anticipating the worst, but sometimes allowing myself to accept the best case scenario.

STEP TWO Taming My Elephant

We sat contemplative in each other's company. Both lost;
tolerating the strangeness of each other's presence. I became
familiar with her moods; and she with my desperate sighs.
Her tears cleared the dirt from her thick skin in streaks, as
I sometimes rested my head on her broad shoulders.

The lines of our relationship shifted. I could not
accommodate her, yet I did not want her to leave. Her absence
would create a vast empty space. I yearned to understand her;
to know more. In the confines of the car, we could not help but
get on top of one another. The radio played and the elephant
sang. At home, she followed me to the pantry where her
hunger quashed my own.

As you might imagine, six tonne elephants have a huge
appetite. In the routine of ordinary life, how could I give her
the attention and nourishment she demanded?

Finite resources were stretched. She grew and filled what
space I could allow her into and I became totally lost in her
underbelly. It became apparent who was consuming whom.

CHAPTER 8

Grief at Play

G race processed her father's death as many children do in those early days; she would ask very direct questions when I was least expecting it. As she climbed out of the car one afternoon, returning from our short drive from day care, she asked, 'Mummy was there a lot of red blood when Daddy died? What did Daddy look like?'

I fumbled for words, my mind went to the blood-stained keys, the accident as it had been described to me. I replied honestly that I did not know. I had chosen not to see Daddy after he had died. Could I reassure her that there was not a lot of blood? She was so little; I did not want her to have bad dreams. But more questions filled my thinking gap: 'Did Daddy drive too fast? How did Daddy's car crash? Where was Daddy going when he died?' I wish I knew the answers. Grace did not cry. She was trying to make sense of something that lacked sense.

We bent the rules quite a bit during this time. She needed me and I needed her. She slept in my bed. I needed that. She watched more TV than usual and we had lots of friends who came to help us. Every night for a month a meal was delivered by a friend or work colleague. Sometimes friends stayed for a while to talk. Words were hard to find. I don't remember much of the content of those conversations, except for one with a colleague I did not know well, who brought brownies.

She stayed for a while, longer than was comfortable. She was a very senior academic psychologist, supervising our team of resident clinical psychologists. I remember she compared my situation to her own, ten years earlier. She had become a single parent to her son in his teens following a difficult divorce. She tried to draw parallels where I found none. While divorce is loss, and single parenting in this context may have some similarities, I felt irritated. Her timing for these simplistic comparisons was all wrong. Mark had died. There would be no more contact; no bitter exchange or opportunity to forgive. Little did she know, my husband had just absconded from our lives and in his footsteps followed a horrific aftermath. I was angry at her suggestion. Mark had not hung around for me to ask why? How? When? I had no answers and the person I should be angry with and shout at was dead. I was left with mess, mess and more mess, and a web of secrets to maintain. I don't think she noticed her error of empathy. We can only ever imagine other peoples' experiences; no two cases are the same. I remained politely distant: the numb widow.

Despite all these kind meal parcels, I had virtually stopped eating. I would feed the children but when I went to the pantry food repulsed me. I survived on a liquid diet. I had loved chocolate, and Mark had left behind a large amount in the cupboard. For the first time it tasted different: indigestible. It and any solid food held no appeal, tasting bitter. The smallest bite incited nausea. I enjoyed the weight loss that ensued, often thinking of the irony that perhaps Mark would have been attracted to my slim non-pregnant physique – he did not like my pregnant or post-pregnancy form. This would be his loss.

My father-in-law had returned with Mark's brother during the first week to finish the 'French doors project'. My husband's battle with perfection had slowed this task to a virtual halt in recent months. Fortunately, his father shares this perfectionism but is also a very able craftsman. For Jack and Tom this was a labour of love. It provided an opportunity to meet, without words, in their grief for Mark. I noted that Tom had replaced his number plate on his car with a dedication plate to his 'lost son' whom he held in high esteem. He was visibly crumpled in his loss. They did not stay for dinner, their task completed they made excuses to leave – 'a long drive home', and Jack would also have to complete the return drive eighteen hours' north the next day. Conversation just clung to the air, strangling thought.

As he was leaving, Tom mentioned that he was still calling Mark's phone, perhaps hoping he would pick up. He asked if I had confirmed that Mark had died, if I'd seen for myself that it was really him. I don't remember the exact words I used but replied that there was no doubt it was Mark. Of course, Tom did not know then the full details of Mark's death, or the day that had preceded it; he was so overwhelmed by his grief, I could not tell him. I needed to protect him from its awfulness.

That night a recurring dream came into my fitful sleep: there was Mark on the mortician's slab; his face and his torso awash with blood, barely recognisable. And a voice of doubt came through: Is this really Mark? Is it Mark that had died? But then, jolted, I would recall the blood-stained keys and doubt dissolved.

Our first weekend after the funeral was difficult. I tried really hard to hold together what was 'normal' for Grace. She had been invited to a birthday party at a local venue. Parties are a big deal in America and often very elaborate even for toddlers: 'A very social occasion.' I often felt self-conscious at these things. For those who had been born and raised in the States, their culture was college football, trips to the beach and poignantly family centred. My family was thousands of miles away and I hated sport; instead preferring a good novel or a country walk. Attending this party meant going out in public for the first time since Mark had died, talking to the other parents and sharing in the happiness of a birthday.

I hate to think how I must have seemed to others: tense, frosty and struggling to communicate. But I could find safe territory by keeping my focus on my children. Joseph was a great prop for distraction; still in his baby sling around my shoulders, taking his afternoon nap. While Grace ran around with all the other princesses and superheroes in costume, I sat in a corner trying hard to blend with the happy wall art. I was holding it all together, and so perhaps were the other parents, undoubtedly dreading treading on razor sharp eggshells.

We dabbled deliberately in superficial conversation until

close to the end, when the cake and a slide show of the party came out. I managed the first verse and chorus of the background track for the slides before becoming overwhelmed by what I was seeing and hearing. On the large white screen were snapshots of our children enjoying the party but it was the words to the overhead music that connected with my emotions and reached down deep inside of me, seemingly ripping me in two. It demanded, consider how many minutes there are in a year of a man's precious life: 60 x 24 x 365 = 525,600. How else can you measure a life? The words flow out ahead of possible thought: a year could be measured in a man's innocent actions, even something as ordinary as a daily cup of coffee; but the most poignant measure of all surely has to be love. 'Seasons of Love' says so much more than I am ready to hear.

I could not cry . . . I could not fall apart here in front of all these people. In a fog I found the door to the deck outside. I slipped away to stand alone and stare straight ahead of me, across the freshly cut grass of the fire station. Private tears fell for all that we had lost; all that Mark had lost. I was so struck by the waste of his life. I was not really sure how I would find my way back to the party. I was visibly shaken and felt disconnected from my body.

But then from the door came a voice. It was time to go home, collect party bags and say thank you to the hosts. I needed to shift into automated mummy mode. I felt momentarily lost and I'm not sure if my distress went unnoticed. The shame of the circumstances, our grief and the feeling of being different rang through me more than ever: not just foreign anymore.

While I was falling apart, I thought Grace was OK; until the next day when life shattered further. I felt confident all was well. It was a hot summer's day and Grace was indoors watching TV when, with a degree of panic in her voice, she called to me that there was a bee. I stopped what I was doing to check this out and observed a fly in the corner of the room. I reassured Grace and continued back to the kitchen in the adjoining room. The next thing I heard were screams. Grace had been stung on the hand by a large wasp. She quickly became hysterical and sobbed inconsolably. The reaction seemed very out of proportion to the assault. I held her and rocked her but I could not provide comfort for her shock that she could be hurt in such a way. She cried out over and over, 'I want my Daddy.'

I was at a loss. How could she be stung by a wasp? Isn't life hard enough? She remembers that 'bee-sting' even now; more than anything. And she is terrified of wasps.

In all the advice and 'rule' books about grief it tells you to not rush into parting with your loved one's possessions or into making big decisions – like moving house or country. I think I broke all those rules! I never questioned my plan to return to England. I needed to escape the goldfish bowl. A close friend told me that in my shoes he would have wanted to run away to Alaska or somewhere remote: to just disappear. I guess I was running – but back to all that was familiar and loved. I felt blessed to have an easy route to start again. And for the first time being of 'another country' held an advantage: I had somewhere to run.

With a firmly held plan to move, even in those first two

weeks, my mum and I began to sort through Mark's clothing and belongings. We took boxes of clothing, books and uniforms to the thrift store just days after Mark died. In a private moment, I concealed an old t-shirt I loved to see him wear in a keepsake box. When I felt love for Mark, I thought, I will hold this and draw in what remains of the smell of him. (Even now, when I hold that shirt, I can just remember what it felt like to be held in his warm embrace.)

Sadly this intimacy was double edged and left me lost at other times. I could not look at photos or my memories of Mark; I did not know who he was. At times, I felt dirty and blemished, and part of my search through his belongings was to uncover the mystery: the untold story of his life.

As the days passed, the turmoil inside me grew. I felt such a conflict of emotions. My internal dialogues would run in circles around my love for the husband I thought I knew and the evidence that was building for a monster of addiction of the worst kind. Remembered conversations began to filter through. Friends had given me a gift certificate for a massage treatment. The spa was a beautiful place; the perfect sanctuary for many. But as I lay on the massage table of the spa, my mind settled on a conversation with Grace the previous summer.

Lying there, purging my mind, I recalled the short ride home from day care. I was heavily pregnant and had been thinking about a brief but difficult phone call with my father earlier that day; made between commitments at work. Dad was now quite muddled and weak; he was barely able to talk on the phone. His lung cancer was getting the better of him. I was anticipating my next trip to England, to be there when he died.

Lost in my own thoughts, a little voice spoke from her seat in the back of the car: 'Mummy, did you know that some children drink from boy's bottoms?'

Struck by her words like a bolt of lightning, I was floored. But to this day I regret my response. I assumed she had heard this at nursery from another child. I told her we don't talk about such things and she did not say another word.

That night, washing up at the sink with Mark after Grace was in bed, I told him what she had said and asked him if he had any idea where she would have heard such a thing. He told me not to worry. He would deal with it, I had enough on my plate. Because I was so overwhelmed and exhausted by my dad's illness, my work and being pregnant, I was so pleased he took responsibility for Grace.

As I lay there now on the cushioned massage table doubt sunk in, my skin began to crawl: Did he let Grace see the pornography? Or did he take this further? If only I hadn't been so consumed by everything else, I might have questioned further where this had come from, and not been so easily reassured by my husband. I doubt a client has ever left a spa more unnerved.

CHAPTER 9

Pieces of a Jigsaw

In our cul-de-sac our closest neighbour, Jan, became one of the few people I felt able to trust both with the children and my confidences. Reluctantly, Jan was also a source of information regarding conversations in the neighbourhood. Following one such conversation I wrote a letter I never felt able to send:

Gossip,
Words can be as sharp as knives, and hurt more. When the
gossip began last week it seems all had forgotten that a man died
who was first a husband and a father before he became the
subject of rumour. As a result of gossip, a four-year-old innocent
child was put at risk of further pain that is irretrievable. She is
hurting enough and it is my job to protect her. When in the Bible
it says that gossiping is in the same league as murder, lying and
prostitution I now understand. You could not have hurt me more

*if you had ripped out my heart with your bare hands. I write this
short note in the hope that next time you feel drawn to gossip and
speculate you will stop and think – think about what you are
gossiping for, its priority and purpose, who does it serve? If you
can do this, I believe the world might be a better place to live.
Thank you.*

In the previous year, Mark had struck up a friendship with a
female photographer, Tammy, who lived a few blocks away. He
had helped her with her computer and, from what he told me,
spent a lot of time listening to her offload about her marital
difficulties. As Mark became more distant when I returned
from trips to England, I had suspected he might be having an
affair with this woman. Friends reassured me this was so
unlikely. I had never met her but apparently she was larger
than life both in personality and physically, and spoke her
mind: not 'Mark's type'.

Not long after Mark had died, Tammy and Jan met at the
school gates. Tammy was central to the local gossip grapevine.
She told Jan that she had suspicions about Mark and was not
surprised that he was a 'paedophile'. Neighbours had observed
that while Grace and I were away in England and Mark was
alone in the house, he had rarely been seen: night or day. Jan
reticently retold to me a story about an occasion when
Tammy's seven-year-old daughter had sat on Mark's lap to
look at the computer. Tammy had noted Mark had an obvious
erection afterwards. Blood rushed from me as I heard this.
Was Mark spending time with Tammy because he could get
access to her daughter? How far would he go to satisfy his
desires? Tammy also remembered Mark making an

inappropriate comment about a neighbour's daughter's pretty budding breasts. I felt so ashamed by his words and actions.

The bottom line of Jan and Tammy's conversation was that Tammy wanted to know if I could return her external hard drive. Mark had been working on helping her organise her data: it was red. I had no idea where this was but presumably the inspector had it. I didn't want Tammy, of all people, to know the details of the investigation. I had to stall for time. I asked Jan to tell her I would look for it when I could face looking through Mark's belongings. This seemed a reasonable delay.

I remembered Mark, in the week before he died, enthusiastically wanting to show me Tammy's photo portfolio on this drive. He told me Tammy had offered to photograph our children at a reduced rate to thank Mark for all his help with her computer. He seemed enthralled by what he saw; I found it all rather boring: endless photos of her children in a variety of settings, standard studio photography. Now, I wonder, was Mark trying to legitimise his involvement with Tammy or his interest in these photos.

The night that Mark met Tammy stands out in my memory. One of our neighbours was celebrating her fortieth birthday at the social club. It was a rare event that Mark and I went out socially. We had arranged to share a babysitter for Grace with Jan's children next door and, although I was on-call, we didn't expect the evening to be interrupted.

But I was working in the hospital that Saturday afternoon and had expected I might be home late. I was to meet Mark at the party, briefly calling in at home to change and make sure

Grace, aged three, was settled next door.

I was already exhausted when I arrived at the party and before I could really relax my pager went off: an urgent call back to the hospital. I was needed on the trauma neurosurgery intensive care unit. A thirty-six-year-old man had been admitted with a severe head injury following a car crash with a drunk driver. When I arrived, this young teacher's wife was at his bedside tightly holding his hand. She turned to look at me as I entered their cubicle; her eyes hopeful that I was bringing some good news.

His face and head were severely distorted from the accident, and cerebral spinal fluid was dripping through the dressings; apart from the ventilator he would not be alive. I held his other hand and looked into his kind eyes as she told me a little of the man who lay before us: an amazing man who had championed youth work in their troubled small-town community. He had been returning from a prayer meeting at their church. It was my job to sit with this young woman and talk her through the next steps: removing the ventilator and allowing her husband to die at peace. He could not recover from his injuries. Although I had encountered many of such tragic situations and been responsible for their care, I found this one particularly upsetting.

It had been a full day: much earlier, I had taken an elderly man with advanced cancer off his life support; this procedure had been interrupted by a call to a young twenty-nine-year-old with severe pain from his leukaemic crisis. Scarcely drawing breath, I next visited John and his partner, a couple I had come to know well. He was in the final stages of HIV disease; there had been new developments and he was gravely ill. I had to tell John he might die in a matter of days. What

seemed like moments later, I was explaining to Steve and
Briony that Steve's tumour had progressed and was now
obstructing his bowel; we had run out of options, we could
keep him comfortable but this was one battle he was not going
to win. He would return home to die in their single wide
trailer.

Sadly this was not an atypical day. It was my job. That
evening, three hours after I'd been paged into the hospital, I
drove home as the darkness came in. I was in no mood to go
out. The layers of the day were taking their toll. I arrived back
at the party but soon realised I could not make small talk with
my neighbours: How was your day? Well, where should I start:
I just watched a young man die? I stared down at the uneaten
canapé on my plate and felt a million miles away from this life.

By my return, Mark had had a few drinks and seemed very
relaxed; which was unusual for him. He did not find parties
and being social came naturally to him. As I approached
Mark, neighbours seemed to compliment me on what a funny
husband I had; they had not seen this side of him. He was a
part of the reckless fun of the party, twisting on the dance
floor with a sombrero on his head. I pulled him aside; I could
smell the alcohol on his breath as he kissed me. 'Mark, I am so
tired. It has been quite a day. I think I am going home.' The
music was loud. The disco lights cast colourful shadows
across the pool outside.

'This is a great party.' Mark shouted to be heard over the disco
beat. 'I haven't had this much fun in ages. Tammy has just gone
to collect some tequila. We are all going to do some slammers. I
can't leave now; I promised ... You don't mind do you? I promise
not to be too late? I won't wake you. You get to bed.'

Feeling very alone, I walked out into the moonlight, grateful for the clear stillness of the stars above me. It was one of nature's halcyon summer nights. I hoped to collect a sleeping child and drop her into bed and then collapse into my own. But it was a day for challenges. Grace was wide awake; she had been fuelled by sweet treats and excitement with the babysitter and Jan's girls. A tantrum ensued as we left, and I was forced to carry her kicking and screaming across the yard. Oh dear, did I feel unwanted, unloved and profoundly sad. What a day it had been.

As I lay in bed, I longed for Mark's support and understanding. I needed him to listen, to hold me and to provide comfort at the end of a terrible day. Instead the bed was empty and I fell asleep trying not to think about my own father amidst all that tragedy. At the time, Dad was having treatment for his lung cancer and I was struggling to keep my own distress separate from all the loss that surrounded me at work. From my knowledge of the type of lung cancer, I knew Dad had only a few months to live. I had a husband who did not do 'loss' or 'dying' and I felt very isolated.

Mark came home in the early hours of the next morning. I later discovered, after several tequila slammers he had escorted Tammy home and stayed for coffee. Mark never drank coffee.

It was readily apparent to me that we needed to talk. We needed some marital counselling if I was going to survive the next few months. We were only skirting around the fact that my father was dying. Mark did not talk about death. His brother, Rick, had died suddenly when he was at air force boot camp, when he was just eighteen years old. He did not go to funerals. He did not ask about my work with the dying or about my feelings when my dad was so ill. He was not surprised, saddened or ashamed when a patient's angry sister shouted 'Kevorkian: murderer' at me after I had spoken with her about withdrawal of life supports. Her brother had defied death for two years in the intensive care unit, fully dependant on the machines; his heart sometimes arrested a half dozen times a day, his kidneys no longer filtered his body's toxins, he was fed via a tube and he could no longer breathe independently. In two years he had not shown any sign of improving or a meaningful response. Although Mark heard my frustration, he could see the parallel the sister had made with Kevorkian - the renowned 'master of euthanasia'. He did not understand nor appreciate the emotional toll of my daily work.

We really were poles apart. My career path had led me to an intimate understanding of death. And for a long time I had felt a human duty to try and comprehend the suffering of others. I believed tears were important and not to be withheld. Mark did not comprehend the concept of empathy. For him, it lacked a point and was too subjective. He had even asked me to give him some phrases so he could empathise. He lacked this language; it was as foreign to him as learning Chinese.

It was in this landscape that our relationship with Faye had begun. A counsellor who also worked as part of our hospital palliative care team, she met with us to try and bridge the gap.

And I now realised there was so much I had failed to comprehend. Time passed anxiously, August arrived and I was still desperate for information that might bring understanding.

Until I had found the post-office key, the inspector seemed quite cagey about the details of their investigation; perhaps, in fairness, he also needed a chance to process the fact that Mark had died and how this might change the direction of his investigation. He could not be persuaded to meet with me any earlier than in the allotted two weeks after our phone call.

Still terrified at what might be implied about my involvement, I took along Greg, the junior associate attorney who was helping me to rewrite my will. He had also looked through the box of remaining computer data on disks and videos we had found at home after the search. I sat nervously in Greg's tank-like SUV, straining to sustain some small talk as we drove downtown to a high-rise office building. I was conscious that this relative stranger already knew quite a lot of personal information about my life. Greg was newly married and a fresh ambitious law graduate who hoped to specialise in corporate law; I wondered what he must think of me. We announced our arrival to the receptionist and waited in a small airless waiting room, not unlike a dental waiting room. I could feel the blood pumping through my heart and yet I felt that if I stood up, I might collapse.

After a few minutes, Inspector Hutton came in to introduce himself. He was in his mid-forties, and reminded me of Mark's own military stiffness, the reliance on protocol. But he was kind and immediately expressed his condolences for my loss. I was struck, as we moved through the corridor of offices, how uninhabited these spaces seemed; how temporary, as if they had forgotten to unpack and would soon be moving on. We passed a room piled high with electronic equipment and he stopped to collect a tray. I recognised that it contained some of our belongings; items removed from our house, all in large Zip-lock plastic evidence bags. We were led to a long grey conference room and invited to sit at the end of the empty table. Another inspector joined us; he had also been present on the day of the raid. After I had explained what I knew about how Mark had died, they described the events of that sorry Wednesday.

They had arrived at about lunchtime, having assumed Mark might be home from work for lunch. They had been observing his activity for several weeks. (I interjected, Mark didn't work; the most he did was go to lectures. They did not know he was a student.) The postal inspectorate was working with the local police force that day. A team of about a dozen officers were deployed to the house as a SWAT team. They had already obtained a warrant from the court to search our home. If Mark had not been home they would have broken in. The police were in full 'SWAT gear' because they were unsure what might await them. They explained that sometimes they are faced with an armed and defensive suspect. They surrounded the house, and Inspector Hutton rang the doorbell. Mark put up no resistance and they went in; and so began their search.

Six officers went upstairs and four into the basement, while two others kept post outside. Slowly and methodically, they swept and searched our home for evidence. Inspector Hutton and his colleague took Mark into the lounge where they relentlessly interviewed him for over five hours. The inspector described Mark as calmly guarded, passively obstructive; at this stage making efforts not to self-disclose or incriminate himself. And yet, Mark did not block them, he did not become at all defensive; quite the reverse, he became disconnected. He handed over his passwords to all his computers and his email. He did not hinder their investigation.

At 5.22 p.m. they left. They recalled that Mark had been eager for them to go before we arrived home, on the premise he needed to run to the grocery store and collect supplies to cook dinner. Inspector Hutton did not suspect that Mark was about to run. He did see him leave the house almost immediately after them and followed them up to the junction with the main road. I wonder: at what point in the afternoon did Mark start to feel like the trapped rabbit? Did they not foresee he would run? Did he always have an escape plan or was he running scared? He was at an end.

What was I doing at 5.22 p.m.? Managing the transfer of two dying patients to the palliative care unit and desperately phoning home to ask Mark to collect our children from day care.

I explained to Inspector Hutton that I was still struggling with gossip in my neighbourhood about what had happened and that I was unsure what more might go 'public'. He reassured me that his officers were discreet and reiterated that both he and the state trooper who had been at the accident scene would not disclose any details to the press. He explained that unfortunately the events of the afternoon were not private. It was impossible to be discreet with a SWAT team all dressed in black bullet-proof uniforms and armed. My neighbours were out in their yards. At that awful moment, as he explained the events in more detail, I realised how much more my neighbours had seen and understood than I had thought. And as I had tried hard to laugh off Mark's absence that terrible afternoon at the day care, Amy the manager had some idea of what I was about to walk into at home – her brother was one of those police officers. He was far from discreet, and would have called his sister to alert her to the events unfolding in the neighbourhood. Did she make the connection?

Unsure if I would be able to hold it all together to ask what I needed to ask, I had written down a list of questions for the inspector, or more simply words to prompt me on a page:

GRACE
P.O. Box
Duration
Extent of involvement/nature of this
Money involved – how is it paid for?
Was there another bank account? Earnings?
Other activities; others involved?
Why?
How?
Who is the typical person who does this?
Red flash drive, Tammy
Computers
Ramifications
What happened that day? Timing?
Mark's demeanour? Regret? Remorse? What he said?
Cell phone calls. Home phone calls. Did they hear my distress?

What a list.

The inspector spent two-and-a-half hours trying to address my questions, as I desperately tried to piece together a sense of who my husband was and understand a world of which I was completely ignorant. I was forcibly opening up my eyes. I was an intelligent, professional woman, but unaware of the world of these horrific crimes against children. Until this conversation, I had clung to the idea that child pornography meant that Mark and others were looking at images on the internet of sixteen-year-old, or at least teenage, girls. My naivety was about to be unravelled: they explained that Mark's interest focused on pre-pubertal girls mostly aged five to eight years.

That went around and around in my head for a while ... five to eight years old ... five to eight years old – our neighbours' girls were all in that age group, our daughter was fast approaching that age group. I had no idea how this worked. Where did you access photographs of girls that young?

Apparently Mark's involvement was extensive. At first, he had joined forums that you could subscribe to; some were from abroad and some based in the USA. Mark had eventually worked his way up in the forum membership by trading images, which was how the forums worked. They assumed he had bought these photos from other sites.

The images were delivered on disc to his post-office box. The inspector and his team had been observing Mark for months after a tip off from the post office about suspect packages arriving for him. They had obtained access to our bank accounts and traced financial transactions for child pornography back to Mark and other individuals. They had discovered that Mark worked for several forums, trading images and helping with website security, so that eventually he had been allowed access to the most extreme photographs that were hidden from the more general membership.

The only monetary outgoing was the initial subscription to each forum and then buying-in images to maintain his position within the forum. Of course, by now I knew he had spent over $15,000 maintaining this addiction. Had he also siphoned off money from our accounts that I was unaware of? Money was always so tight. We lived from pay cheque to pay cheque despite my generous medical salary. Were there loans I did not know existed? Mark had over a terabyte of pornographic material. What can a 'terabyte' store? It sounds large. Two computers full of the stuff were removed from his office.

Two computers: another penny drops. Mark had bought several new extra computers in the last year which he had told me were for his contract work, provided by Skip, briefly his employer until he was dismissed. I did not need to have, nor had, any access to them. The inspectors asked me if I had had any suspicions that something was wrong. I explained that all of this was new and foreign to me and everything came as a complete shock.

I clarified what I knew: we were struggling in our marriage and I had found Mark increasingly distant and perhaps depressed. He had been spending a lot of time on his computer, but I had assumed he was applying for jobs. Mark had been unemployed while completing his MBA. A contract job had come to an abrupt end and he had even pretended to me for a short while he was still going out to work. I had assumed that his loss of self-esteem and loss of hope were the result of feeling he could not measure up to nor provide for his physician wife and family. Little did I know that he was busy in the basement, working for these forums into the early hours. No wonder he had not found a job with this level of distraction. His efforts were feverishly employed elsewhere.

Top of my list was my concern for Grace; my anxieties were only made worse when I heard the age of the girls that Mark's collection of images suggested he was most addicted to. Inspector Hutton asked me if I had any reason to suspect Mark's relationship with Grace was anything but ideal: did any concerning behaviours come to mind?

I desperately wracked my brain for possible suspicious links. I remembered a time when Mark had looked after Grace for the afternoon; she was two years old, and I had gone to visit a friend who had just had a baby. Mark had encouraged me to leave Grace behind; it was the first time she had been left completely alone in his care. When I arrived home it was a hot and humid summer day; Mark and Grace were in the backyard. They were having a fun time. Grace was running around playing with the garden hose. She was naked. Charmed by her joy, Mark had taken a photograph of her. Later, he had this image on the wall in his office. I remember the photo had faded in the direct sunlight through the window and had developed an angel-like quality which we had both loved.

A further niggle of concern was raised in me. Please no, not Grace. But both inspectors doubted the significance of this story. Many parents took such innocent photographs, which held no significance in their world. They reassured me that they had not come across pictures of Grace; as far as they could recall. They had watched hours of videotape of her dancing in the living room or singing without suspicion, just smiles. To further reassure me, they described how one man they had investigated had put white duct tape around his computer tower on the floor, demarcating where one life ended and another began. Mark had two computer towers in his office; one for home and another for the dark life he was leading. To the inspectors, this suggested he too kept a clear line of division between the two lives. They did not feel the need to suspect Mark of 'home grown' child pornography.

Slightly contradictory, though, was their account of how this addiction had begun. I naturally wanted to know. A question burning inside me was how long had Mark been doing this? And in particular, did these behaviours pre-date his relationship with me? The inspector attempted to describe two kinds of addict; the first was habitual-endogenous; someone who from the beginning always liked this kind of stimulation and needed it for sexual arousal. The second type of internet paedophile became habituated to worsening degrees of pornography over time. These were the circumstantial addicts: a separation from a partner or a loss of sexual intimacy with a partner over time, or readily available pornographic material would provoke this slippery slope, and as the addiction was cultivated and fed it might become more severe.

It was the extent of Mark's addiction that had led Inspector Hutton to suspect he was not just a circumstantial addict. It went too far and too deep for that. Although the activity they had traced only dated back six months, what was clear was Mark knew what he was doing and had developed an instrumental role for himself in the forums he had joined. Did this merely reflect his expertise in computers or was this the result of an accumulation of knowledge and a longer term desire for the extremes of pornography?

Two versions of the same story are played out in my head.
The first is that Mark became addicted to pornography the
summer after his operation on his spinal cord and this was
then compounded by his staying behind during my six-month
sabbatical in England with Grace. This theory lends itself to
my guilt: an absent wife, a slippery slope. It is very believable.

The other story is not much better. Mark never loved me,
because he couldn't. He loved young girls before he met me.
Perhaps for a short while in the early stages of our marriage,
before babies, he was able to quash this urge. It was Faye's
observation that I had a child-like naivety, believing the best
and unexposed to the realities of life. Even physically, I had not
changed since my teen years and, on our wedding night, I
recall that Mark had delighted in the Shirley Temple ringlets
that fell to my shoulders. But then babies came along, my body
changed and I looked less like a child. I became more like a
woman: one who had just had two babies. During pregnancy,
and certainly afterwards breast feeding, he lost interest and
the addiction re-emerged. Could I even be convinced that for
Mark being married to a doctor was a good meal ticket? That I
was financially able to feed his habit and because I was so
innocent to this ugly world, so trusting and so unsuspecting of
his night time habits: I was the ideal wife.

I remained fearful of the ramifications of Mark's actions. It
was painfully clear that Inspector Hutton had not expected
Mark to die. As a courtesy, he asked my 'permission' to
continue to allow them to assume Mark's internet identity.
They had begun an effort to ensnare others who were in
contact with Mark. They had been answering his emails and
now could also check his mailbox until it ceased to be active. I

was advised not to try to log into Mark's email accounts; I
advised them I wouldn't be able to anyway. I had never had
knowledge of his passwords for either of his computers, nor
had I any notion of other levels of computer security.

Fear still consumed me; I needed reassurance that I was not
about to be arrested or charged in connection with these
crimes. They assured me that the case against Mark was
closed. Their ongoing investigations would be helped by the
information they had collected from his computers and their
ongoing activity in his persona, but that was all. The inspector
expressed that there was likely to be some good from all of
this: some more arrests. Inspector Hutton would let me know
if there were any developments in the information they
uncovered. He gave me his card and advised me to call if I
needed to. They would let me know when they would return
the remainder of the computer equipment; the majority of the
data had already been removed and I could have all the
camera equipment back. I was handed several clear 'crime
scene' bags of equipment that they had seized from our home.
In their minds, my part in this had come to a close.

I don't remember the conversation that followed in the car
home. I was in a state of shock. I am sure I did make polite
conversation – what do you say after that? The volume of
pornography in our home was unimaginable, the potential
content unfathomable and the reassurances I had been given
did not provide any comfort. My fear that Mark's addiction
knew no bounds had only escalated. My assumptions had
been quashed and the rumours of 'a paedophile preying on
neighbourhood children' seemed more likely. The excuses I

had been trying to make for Mark and his behaviour no longer rang true. I began to wonder again if Mark had hurt our children; was he capable of suicide and risking the life of another man?

Mark, quite believably, could easily have lived two lives; there was plenty of evidence to support this rationalisation. After all, Mark had essentially been living in duplicity. He was a very black-and-white character, a concrete thinker in every essence of the word. Mark could rationalise his actions with what seemed to him viable excuses.

I remember a conversation that we had had the previous year about 'virtual' pornography. I had been listening to the radio on the way home from work where they had been discussing if society should tolerate pornographic images that are artistically created by computer software. No children are used in the production of this material: some argue therefore that this is art not pornography. I was appalled. How could anyone think this was acceptable? Mark gave the counterargument.

Earlier that year, I had encountered a child protection dilemma at work. A patient on our ward was dying from cancer of the gallbladder. Jenny had a seven-year-old daughter who was being cared for by her partner of several years while she was in hospital. As I talked to Jenny one day on my morning rounds, she enthusiastically described how attentive a father her partner had become for her daughter. She described how he would sit in the bathroom while the young girl bathed, listening to her worries. The door was closed. At first I was not at all suspicious but then, encouraged by other members of the team, I asked Jenny a few more questions. I felt torn. I did not want to burden Jenny with the idea that her partner might be abusing her daughter. Others had no doubt. I did not want Jenny to be the subject of gossip and speculation. I felt it was wrong to upset her daughter by throwing them into territory of the child protection team. She might be removed from her family home into a place of safety at a time when she was just about to lose her mother. Had she not suffered enough?

I came under pressure to do what was right: to follow my suspicions. I made the call. A team went to the house and removed Jenny's daughter. She was taken to her aunt's home where she remained. Jenny had become confused from liver failure and died, without knowledge of these events, just forty-eight hours later.

I had wanted to believe we had done the best in this case and I talked it over with Mark. He was appalled at the conclusions my team had come to about this man. He wanted me to believe in the best intentions of Jenny's partner. How could anyone harm a vulnerable child about to lose their mother? It was unimaginable.

STEP THREE Elephant Down

Terror descended in a moment. Isolated from her herd, I had stepped into my elephant's new found territory. She too knew fear, anger and terror. Vulnerable, she attempted to charge and I was covered in her dirt and dust; the ground beneath us shook with an almighty tremble.

As she fell, I was carried with her. Some could hear the echo of our cries and the earth shake at our point of impact.

It was then that I saw her pain; she had been hurt. Ensnared in a trap, she could not run. She tore down structures as her flailing limbs cut through the air before thundering to the floor. My own injuries in her distress were far from minor. She rocked her hulking mass.

Slowly though, as I lay stunned, she became an immoveable block; pinning me down.

Days passed before she took her last breath, clinging on to life in the wilderness. We lay silent as life sapped away.

Friends lifted me from her wreckage. What now? I needed to take courage: my challenge had just begun.

CHAPTER 10

Widow Stamped and Supported

The day of my appointment at the social security office to register Mark's death arrived in the midst of this maelstrom. I arrived early at the downtown location and I sat alone in the car with a coffee. My legs felt like lead, paralysed by the thought of going inside. My experiences of bureaucracy to date had not been good. On earlier occasions, Mark was always around to help me navigate the system. Today, I was there because of him: to make his death official.

It was not really clear what I should do when I went inside the highly-guarded government building. I took a paper raffle ticket and waited for my turn in the queue. There were a lot of people waiting, and a number of those already being seen appeared to be in heated dispute over the benefits they were attempting to claim. When I finally made it to the counter, the lady at the booth seemed irritated that I had 'clogged up the queue'. No one had explained that I did not need a ticket. I would be called when they were ready as I had a pre-booked appointment. I sat back down in the noisy and crowded waiting area. It was an uncomfortable wait.

Eventually, I was called to a booth in the back room: a large office space separated by cardboard dividers. The clerk was curt and seemed inconvenienced by my loss. I was asked to repeat the information that I had already provided on the phone for each member of our family: Mark, myself, Joseph and Grace. She struggled with my very English accent. Standing, she then crossed the room to copy the death certificate. I was left anxiously shifting in the hard plastic seat. The air-conditioning felt cool on my neck and provided relief from the scorching September heat outside. She returned to her desk, where with the efficiency of a robot, she informed me of the benefits which would be paid to the children and I as a result of Mark's death. She was obligated to read out loud every word of the content of the lengthy paperwork; it was printed in capital letters, except for the dates. She commanded me to sign to confirm the truth.

... THE DECEASED AND SURVIVING SPOUSE WERE LIVING IN THE SAME ADDRESS AT THE TIME OF DEATH.
THE DECEASED WAS LAST MARRIED TO ALICE WELLS ON August 15th, 1998 IN THE UK, BY A CLERGYMAN OR PUBLIC OFFICIAL. THE MARRIAGE ENDED BY DEATH ON July 25th, 2007.

'THE MARRIAGE ENDED BY DEATH ON July 25th, 2007.' 'THE MARRIAGE ENDED ...' This one sentence remained suspended in time as it reverberated around my head.

Until it was read out loud, I had not thought of my marriage as no longer existing. There it was in capital letters and large font on crisp white paper. I was not thinking of my marital status in past tense. I wore both my wedding and engagement ring; on this day, I wanted to be the 'ordinary' wife, married to Mark. I wanted to feel close to him. This interviewer now asked me to acknowledge that I was 'no longer married'. I wanted to say no, I won't sign. I don't want to 'not be' married: I am married. Suddenly, it seemed so final. To claim the $260 widow's benefit, I had to sign away my marriage in that moment. It was over. It was worth no more than $260; finished in a one-off payment.

This rather indifferent representative of the social security office was only the beginning of a very trying relationship. The children's benefits were quite considerable: a monthly support allowance. I was informed they could not claim this if I left the country with them. It felt as if I was being judged for removing them from the US.

Barely able to breathe, I returned to the car; it had become a frequent place of refuge. I sat there and fell to pieces. I don't know how long I sobbed for. My whole body ached as I grieved for the loss of my husband, my marriage and the future I had dared to imagine for our family. I felt very alone in that moment in the busy concrete-blocked parking lot.

About five days after Mark had died, mixed in with the bereavement cards, insurance forms and bills came several letters from local widow and bereavement support groups and counsellors. They had picked up my contact information from the funeral announcement in the newspaper and the rest had been provided by the phone book or funeral parlour. Seeing these solicitations, I felt it might be best to try other sources of support, because Faye knew me at work. What followed was really a catalogue of disasters. I was desperate to make sense of my situation and find some peace.

My first attempt to 'clarify' came too soon; about a week after the accident, at my own insistence. I paid through the roof to see a 'Christian' counsellor who had some expertise in marital therapies and loss. An hour was spent literally charting the events, as we knew them, on a large wall-mounted whiteboard. The counsellor theorised about Mark and his behaviours. He then tried to create structure and clarity where none really could be found. Wide generalisations were made very quickly and from all that I remember, apart from some initial storytelling, I don't think I did much of the talking. The board was wiped clean at the end of our one-hour consultation. This had been an unhelpful introduction to bereavement support, and I emerged more distraught and several hundred dollars worse off.

Following the trauma at the social security office, and as I emerged from my initial fog of grief, I decided to try a widows' group. I hoped perhaps to find someone young and widowed with children who could relate to the weight of parenting in this state. My heart sank at the first meeting. While the other widows and widowers were all very welcoming and delighted to see me there seeking their help, it was not the right group for me. I was too recently bereaved, too young, bereaved by sudden death and all that was without reaching deeper into the depths of my true story of loss. The other participants had so much in common; the average age was seventy and their marriages had been lengthy and the impact of their loss over time was great. They spoke of feeling cheated that their spouse had died first and of the wonderful years of marriage they had shared. My story was so different. I'm not sure who was more embarrassed: they because my husband was too young to die; or me because I was thirty years their junior and my experience of married life too brief to be among these widows. I felt so far from this term 'widow', I wanted to rail against it; and yet at times it seemed as though I was weighed down by a large 'w' tattooed on my back that everyone could see and might lead them to cross the road to avoid awkward conversation. I tried to make it work in this group. I attended twice before concluding it was not right for me. I was referred on to a younger session.

The next, and final, group was probably the greatest disaster. I found that the facilitator for this large gathering of 'young widows' was very pushy. After an introductory phone call, she did seem to recognise that it would be difficult for me not to disclose all that was going on 'behind the scenes' and still be an active participant 'in the group'. She asked permission to tell the group a little of my loss: 'just the grief bit'. She liked to give her own summary of each person's story.

The evening of the first meeting arrived; I was hopeful that this might be the right meeting for me. Maybe here in this venue I would meet someone who shared some features of my loss. After some gawky time stood pushing lettuce and a bread roll around a plate, the time for awkward social introductions passed and we all gathered seated in a circle. I was very nervous. I could see already that among even this group of 'young' widows, I was the youngest by about fifteen years. I concluded that 'young' was a loose term intended to mean less than seventy and not necessarily retired. I still stood apart. Furthermore, as I glanced around the room trying not to make eye contact with any of my fellow participants, I recognised a few of the other faces from the hospice unit where I worked. I had helped navigate some of these people through their loved one's illness and their initial grief. I was someone from the other side of their loss.

Nothing prepared me for how trapped I felt as the formidable facilitator, Pearl, went around the group checking in with everyone. She insisted on some form of summary of the week's events and challenged participants if they said they were 'alright' if she thought otherwise. I was saved until last. Pearl's words trapped me in a web of deceit and intrigue from that point onward: 'Alice is here because her husband died in a car accident. She does not want to discuss the circumstances and we should not ask her anything about her husband's death; it is still under investigation.' And with those words she perhaps thought she had closed the door on speculation. I attended this group just a handful of times.

However, when I went to a group I had an evening 'for me', and that gave me breathing space. Each time I had a babysitter for the children; she collected them from day care, fed them and put them to bed. I had the early evening before the group to have some quiet time away from life as it was: my kids, forging a way forward and work. I would sit in Starbucks, just a few minutes from the meeting hall, and develop my addiction to their chai tea: simple things provide great comfort. This sweet spiced tea had by now become my main dietary intake. Throughout this time of searching for a group, I think I was really searching for someone with a similar story.

Someone who had walked in my shoes, who really would understand, someone who had charted this territory and survived; and could tell me how to move forward. To this day, I haven't found that person; in those weeks and early months I felt very alone.

I spent most of this time feeling like a different kind of widow who fitted nowhere: fully informed, well versed on the subject of bereavement, supported by a multidisciplinary team who provided the ideal bereavement support, but traumatised, shamed, dirty, betrayed, bewildered, loved and yet unloved, and foreign; in so many senses of that word.

At one point, my desperate search led me to call a friend whose son had committed suicide following a struggle with drug addiction. I hoped he would tell me how I should feel; and, perhaps, how to cope with the shame of a death that did not meet people's poetic and romantic speculations. It had started to feel like a storyboard would run in people's heads that did not bare any resemblance to my reality. A tragic story of a young widow, who lost her husband in a terrible car crash, perhaps she too was injured at the scene; two young children without a devoted father and a memory of his presence in their short lives. For years, the story people told themselves would trap me, almost as much as the reality itself. I would feel like I was living a life of deceit. Even today, I have moments of duplicity. But what I understand now is that we are all like this: showing in each encounter only the parts of ourselves we feel safe or need to show.

My friend helped me to wrestle with the thought that Mark may have committed suicide, which quite simply I will never know with any certainty. Regardless, I am similarly left with a feeling of guilt: could I have prevented his death? And the lack of a time of reckoning: he left no note and no opportunity to question, understand or forgive. I realise now I was beginning a painful process of reconciliation with what I knew of the truth that would take years. First accepting that Mark had died, and then the nature of his death and all that led to those final moments and extended beyond them. It was and is a slow process, requiring considerable patience with and compassion for myself.

STEP FOUR The Wrong Tools

Assembling the right tools for this formidable task needed time. I would like to say I took the time to survey the beast at my feet. That is what I should have done. I was approached by wise men with foolish advice. Experienced elephant hunters were keen to share their tried and tested approaches.

But remember: no rules apply. Tenacity, patience, wisdom, companionship, isolation and courage were all required in fair measure. Each of us must find our own way with the smallest of spoons and the strongest of stomachs. Sometimes a blunt instrument is all that we have to hand.

Space was essential, as was time. A trusted team gathered who were determined, loyal, patient, forgiving and who listened. We all learnt that sometimes just being and not doing was enough.

Sing – let the soul have its voice. The belly of the elephant provided a great acoustic in which to yell, cry and create new melodies.

I needed to remember not to compare or draw parallels; as did those around me. No one elephant is the same as another.

These creatures are quite unique in their complexity.

Progress is not a word that you can befriend. It will only bring you frustration. Instead, expect hurdles and setbacks. Just as I did, with your own elephant, you may have to climb right into the gut of the matter and get dirty in the far dark recesses of this carcass. Sweat and tears may be your only reward.

CHAPTER 11

Emesis

Labor Day marks the end of the summer, and is a time when families come together to share a meal and company. For us, that summer, it marked a long four-day holiday weekend. Our family had been blown apart, and without our friends as a buffer we felt very vulnerable. I was greatly relieved when Kate and her husband asked us to join them for dinner at their friends' house. I was worried about my ability to be 'social', as I had barely left the house in weeks, but I knew it would be good for Grace to be with other children.

We were made to feel very welcome and it was the first time I felt relaxed and even felt I could laugh – it was funny how even cracking a smile felt somehow dishonourable in the midst of our grief. At last carefree, Grace darted about with the other children dressing up in a variety of costumes; no princesses but plenty of knights and firefighters. Much to my surprise, we stayed late into the evening, returning home to put Joseph to bed. We had remembered how to have fun.

I had not long been in bed when I heard a sound of distress from Joseph's cot: he was throwing up. And so it started, the most violent vomiting, which didn't stop until the following evening. Grace seemed fine, so Clare took her to nursery. In the midst of Joseph's sickness, our realtor called: could a potential buyer come and view the house in thirty minutes! Life became farcical at this point. Everywhere I looked there were piles of dirty sheets and towels from the sickness, but I didn't dare say 'no' in case this was the viewing that would sell the house. I ran around trying to find a place to conceal my washing in the garage and with a spray disinfectant for all the door knobs. I needed to be sure we did not spread our misery; surely they would not buy a house where they contracted a horrid stomach virus.

An added complication was where would I take Joseph while they viewed the house? We were required to be out of the house, it is the American way of viewings. The thought of keeping a vomiting baby in the car at the end of the road, while we waited, did not seem a good idea. Mercifully, Kate thought that they might have been the source of the virus, and feeling suitably guilty offered for us to wait at their home, just around the corner. And so I bundled Joseph with buckets, towels and wipes into the car and we turned out of our street as the viewing couple arrived. I prayed that they would not suspect or fall prey to the dreaded 'bug'.

At this point I began to feel dreadful, and that evening, by the time Joseph had stopped vomiting, my own sickness began and did not relent for two days. It was becoming increasingly difficult to know where to turn. I had this sinking feeling that

I had called in more favours than I was due. Ordinarily, a family will muddle through an illness like this, restricting contact with others so that you don't pass the dreaded illness on. A husband, just as Mark had done a year before, will hopefully relieve his wife of childcare duties so that she can have the space to be unwell. I was already physically weak and barely eating when the vomiting struck, and I quickly felt faint and came close to blacking out. Again friends ran out for fluids and to collect Grace from nursery, passing each over the threshold of the front door, while trying to keep their distance from the contagion itself. As soon as I could send Joseph back to nursery I did. And just as there seemed to be a window to recover myself, there was a telephone call to say Grace was vomiting at pre-school.

That afternoon, Grace lay sleeping on the sofa, while I was collecting up washing and changing dirty beds. As I came back in to check on her, she began to call out. I put my arms around her, she did not seem to be awake, but began to speak and gesture. She had a terrified look in her eyes and did not register my presence at all. She was trying desperately to curl up into a ball, like a frightened animal, while calling out, 'Keep the blood away from me.' She was petrified. Her reaction was so physical. She was pale and sweating. Despite my presence and telling her, 'It's alright, Mummy's here,' she remained in a trance of terror. She frantically rubbed her legs, saying, 'No, no, please no.' It was as if, to her, our red-patterned Egyptian carpet had become a wild river of blood, lapping up close to her ankles and ready to engulf her in its path. But after a few minutes, she seemed to come to and cuddled into me, before falling back into a peaceful sleep.

I was shaken by Grace's apparent horror. It felt as if, for a moment, I had a window into her distress and the impact Mark's death had had on her. Until this point, there had only been minimal hints; some tears, a few tantrums, occasional questions searching for an understanding of what had happened in the accident, but nothing out of the ordinary for your average four-year-old whose father had just died. In these few moments, I saw a fear that I knew in my heart changed the meaning of Mark's death for all of us. It seemed to point to the fact he had abused her. And yet, I could rationalise her cries: a nightmare caused by fever, nuanced by her limited understanding of Mark's accident. Surely, this was not so unusual.

Struck by the pressures of time, I realised I could not gather Grace up to go to nursery to collect Joseph; I needed to find someone to stay with her while I dashed out. Feeling very vulnerable, I stepped outside and looked up the street: I would have to ask a neighbour to help me. Until then I had successfully avoided even eye contact with my close neighbours. A few had dropped off gifts for the children and cards. They had tried to reach out but I felt very exposed in their presence. But now I had to ask and, of course, they were happy to be able to do something to help. A neighbour kindly came in and sat with Grace while she slept; I had to trust. As I drove away, I hoped and prayed that Grace would stay asleep, and she did. The rest of the evening passed without event. Grace stopped vomiting and somehow we all made it to bed.

For a few nights, Grace slept in my bed, where I could be sure she was alright. That night marked the first occasion that I had a vivid feeling that Mark had returned. Half-light was creeping in, and Grace lay sleeping next to me. Suddenly, I was conscious of someone standing at the door of the bedroom. It was Mark holding a tray of tea and toast. Ironically, I can count on one hand the occasions he had brought me breakfast in bed in our nine years of marriage. It was a rare and special treat. Now, I was struck with anger and irritation. I whispered, 'Don't be so ridiculous Mark, can't you see she has been vomiting. We don't need toast right now.' The vision was so real that for a moment, I was confused and struggling to make sense of what was happening. 'How can you be alive? What a mess to come back to. Please just go, leave us, you are making it all worse.' As reality took a hold again, I found myself shaking, tears convulsing through my body. And then I lay still waiting for the morning to come, as had become the norm. I rarely slept beyond 4 a.m.

Grace stirred, dreaming as I lay there in the half-light. I was suddenly jolted from my own distress as she began to mutter in her sleep. She sat up and began rubbing her legs again, obviously disturbed by some sense of what she felt was on them. She then sleepily muttered, 'No it's all sticky, get it off me! I don't want that cream on me . . . no . . . no!'

'Grace, what is it? Mummy's here, it's OK. There's nothing there. It's a dream.'

She said no more and yet had said everything in that moment. Her sleepy distress dispersed and she went back to sleep. I crept into the bathroom once I was sure she was peaceful. Closing the door to, I climbed into the shower where I knew that I could cry without disturbing anyone.

Standing there as the water poured down and washed away my tears, I knew from that moment that Mark had abused

Grace. My worst fear was now a reality. My mind began to race again: Where? How? How much? When? If these experiences were coming out in her dreams then was she thinking about them? How hadn't I known? Because I really hadn't known.

The pieces of the jigsaw began to fit, but nevertheless made no sense. What was the bigger picture? As I stayed there in the shower paralysed by my thoughts, I prayed to God: 'Please Lord, no more. I cannot take anymore. Help me to help my children.'

The next day I took Joseph to nursery; a miraculous calm enabled the morning routine, with Grace staying at home with me. But as that well-known phrase attests: 'it never rains but it pours.' It was not long before the nursery phoned to say that Joseph was vomiting again and could I collect him. Once again the practical took over, and the nightmare that was by now fully unravelling became the backdrop. Duvet days were never an option; and perhaps it is God's saving grace that at this point there was little time to dwell in thoughts.

I took Grace to the doctor, who reassured me that these semi-hypnotic delirious episodes were likely to be associated with the virus we had all had and he found her physically to be OK. But I wasn't really worried about the physical. I knew in my gut there was more.

And I wanted my suspicions to be all wrong but I knew, as did those I had confided in, that the events of the previous day had only confirmed my horrifying earlier concerns.

Have you ever wished you could open up your child and read them like a book? I desperately wanted to be the fly on the wall to my child's experiences. As part of my medical training, I had received instruction in how to approach situations of suspected sexual abuse. I knew it was important not to push the child further than they are ready to talk about and that it is really important not to ask leading questions. I also knew that Grace was more likely to confide in me than anyone else at this point. The weight of this responsibility and my own emotions, as you can imagine, went beyond hefty.

I sought advice about how to approach a conversation with Grace. And I delayed, comforting myself with the thought that I had to find the right moment, or that perhaps this was unnecessary; perhaps I had it all wrong.

Grace loved our Jacuzzi bath, but she was not really big enough to venture in alone. And so, in these chaotic days of people coming and going, the occasional bubble brimming bath together allowed a certain intimacy that we needed. The bath provided the quiet space I needed to venture into this terrifying conversation with my little girl.

'Grace, Mummy has been thinking about something you said a long time ago, last year when Mummy was pregnant. Do you remember when you told me, when we were in the car, that sometimes children drank from their daddy's bottoms?'

This time the story flowed out.

'Yes Mummy, I saw pictures on Daddy's computer. He showed me them.'

Calm . . . calmly, I replied, using her own words, 'Daddy showed you some pictures?'

'Yes, we looked at them together sometimes when you were upstairs with Joseph or at work.' It all tumbled out, 'Daddy told me not to tell you because he thought you might get upset or cross. It was our secret.'

'Grace, I'm not cross with you. All of this makes me very sad, but can you tell me if anything else has happened with Daddy?'

There was more. 'It is OK Mummy; Daddy says it makes boys happy, so it was OK Mummy.' She paused. 'I don't think I should say anything Mummy, Daddy said it would upset you, I don't want to upset you. I promised Daddy.'

We needed to go on. 'Grace, Daddy has died now and it is really important that you and I don't have secrets because Daddy isn't here for you to talk about this anymore.'

Slower now, the detail beyond words gingerly creeps out: 'On the stairs, it was sticky . . . white creamy stuff.'

And then my darling four-year-old daughter gestures, in a way no child could if they have not experienced or seen masturbation. Innocent reassurance came as my face perhaps hinted to my horror, 'It was alright Mummy. It made Daddy and the other boys happy.'

I find words. 'Grace, Mummy is very sad that this happened. What Daddy did was wrong. But you have done nothing wrong. I love you and I am sad because I wish I had known before. Please, let's not have any more secrets. Is there anything else you can tell Mummy?'

'No Mummy, can I get out now?' The bath was getting cold. The bubbles had lost their magical glow.

I settled Grace into bed, and it amazes me to this day that I remained calm. I did not cry and incredibly the conversation had the same tone as conversations we have had about the ingredients list on back of the cereal packets at the breakfast table – 'What is a carbohydrate Mummy?' – not the abuse of my precious innocent child.

At that moment, when Grace opened the door on her abuse, I so wanted to push further, to know the details: How much? How far? How often? 'Just' Daddy? This strangling desire to know more and to somehow wipe the slate remains with me today. This has to have been the greatest lesson in patience a person would have to endure. In what has been nine years now, we have had four short conversations about her abuse. I have barely made it beyond the 'foreword' of her book. It is often said that it is the unknown that is most fearful. We can act on what is known, begin to repair, talk and support. But without a frame to put this on, I feel powerless to do anything and so I am left with a choice between fear and faith; I'd like to say I choose faith.

Inspector Hutton had not expected to hear from me at this point. Out of town on another investigation, thankfully, he answered his phone. I explained recent events; he reassured me again nothing had suggested domestic child sexual abuse. But he promised to repeat the search of the data retrieved from Mark's computers, this time using the serial number codes from our cameras. Clare organised a meeting with our own paediatrician and spoke to a coordinator at the regional child abuse support centre, who agreed to meet me 'if' it was necessary. The professionals seemed sceptical of my suspicions.

One of my favourite aspects of my job was my work as an ethics consultant. The messiest cases in the hospital came my way to mediate and clarify. Sometimes getting to the point of understanding meant reaching back to the wisdom of great and ancient philosophers. In the Myth of Sisyphus, one of my favourite philosophical tales, Sisyphus pushes a large boulder uphill; such is the hard monotony of his life – one step forward two steps back. Unlike my friend Sisyphus, I think at this point my boulder was free falling and taking me with it. What would I have given for a little monotony, but I am missing the point of Sisyphus's tale: he was suffering greatly in his monotony and lack of progress. Sometimes, my patients and their families have to wait weeks for the results of tests: it is the waiting that erodes away at their souls. Once again, I too began the waiting game of trying to reach the experts for a plan and reassurance, where there might be none. Living with any degree of uncertainty can wreak havoc with the heart.

In the middle of the afternoon, just a few days later, the call came. Alone in the house, I sat down on the sofa as the weight of what I was hearing on the telephone played around in my head.

'I am really sorry Mrs Wells, when we ran a search on your family's main camera we found over 800 images of Grace that were of a pornographic nature.' Surely everyone knows bad news should be delivered face to face.

'Oh my, oh my . . .' I could not breathe. I was lost. 'What kind of things?'

'There were photos of Grace in her dressing-up clothes: Cinderella, Sleeping Beauty, and perhaps adult lingerie.' This turned out to be my own tied around her. 'There were no images of penetrative sex but it appears your child was coaxed to act out oral sex and perform acts of male oral sex and masturbation.'

I was numb. My brain made a leap: Could the horror be worse? Grace's own words – 'other boys' – came to mind. I asked him, 'Was it just Mark?'

A short pause. 'We didn't find any images of other people with Grace, but we did find an image that was stored with your daughter's pictures. It had been coded in the same way, another girl filed as 'Lisa Marie', in March 2005. Does this mean anything to you?'

In March 2005, I was in England for five days with Grace, interviewing for a general practice training post for the following September. I was preparing to take the six-month sabbatical to complete my British training. In what was a quick turnaround, we flew back home, I changed suitcases before flying out to Santa Fe for a conference. Grace was now left in Mark's care for three days; it was the first time she had not travelled with me.

Is that where Lisa Marie fitted in? Grace's photo's dated back to when we had returned from England: spring 2006. The grooming process began in March of that year and the photo's evolved in type over the following sixteen months until Mark's death. Inspector Hutton felt that as there was no legal case to be made against Mark, Grace did not need to be examined and interviewed about her experiences. Fear grabbed me. I could only believe that it did not end here. There was more to uncover. I was on a sharply defined slippery slope. I came off the phone and my body collapsed beneath me. Alone, I sat stunned by what I had heard. I felt in that moment that I could not endure any more: I was in a living hell.

I closed my eyes, tears still flooding down my face. In the darkness, I had a vision and the sense of a voice lifting me up. There, quite clearly in my mind's eye, was Jesus nailed to a cross, surrounded by light, his hands were pierced and bleeding. Where there seemed no path to understanding, I knew in that moment with all of my consciousness that only he understood my pain. I found myself knowing with unwavering certainty that he knew my suffering and had felt worse. Furthermore, understanding came: God felt worse as he watched his son die from this barbaric death. They knew and understood my suffering and would provide me comfort in the darkness to come. Calm came over me and somehow I was able to carry on. I knew someone understood my living hell. I did not need to find a widow like me.

As I shared the latest information with my closest friends and family, some were shaken with disbelief and others had their own suspicions confirmed. They had arrived at this conclusion before me. Even in the limited individual sessions Mark had spent with Faye, she had wondered what was really going on for this man. She had found him argumentative, avoidant and unable to connect with feelings and express what he felt. He had danced a circus around individual planned appointments with her and when joining us for a couple's session had sat apart from me, rigid in the armchair, distrusting what he saw as an alliance already formed between myself and Faye.

From the little that Mark did reveal, it was apparent that he was intimidated by the intensity of my relationships with others; especially my family. He had always expected that I would fall in love with America and not want to leave, but he feared I would ultimately leave him or perhaps not return from a trip to the UK. He felt insecure. He did not feel that I would ever put him 'top of my list'.

I had no list. We would often find ourselves arguing around this point and indeed had done so not long before he died. I do not believe Mark really wanted to leave his country. He would argue however that one day he would make the ultimate sacrifice and cross continents for me. But the goalposts kept moving until one day, I cracked. I argued that I had put him first: I had moved continent. If he needed evidence of my sacrifice, he needed look no further than my not being home when my father was dying. It was one of the few arguments Mark could not win. My father's death marked a turning point; leaving me more determined than ever of my need to return home and Mark at a loss for how to resist. I was grieving for my family. In my work with the dying, I had learnt how a membrane sits around the bereaved before and after the illness; did Mark sit outside that membrane? What did this mean for us? In May 2006, at a time when we knew my dad was going to die, Mark's relentless credit card spending on pornographic material escalated beyond belief.

Despite all that was now unravelling in my private life, I had now had six weeks of leave and it was time for me to return to work. It was a busy time for me: completing paperwork for social security, probating, working out our losses and selling our home and belongings to move back to England. I resumed mostly academic and teaching duties, struggling with the demands of the clinical work. The knowledge of the circumstances of Mark's death was kept to just those close; a selective few who needed to know. I feared what people would think or say if the truth became known. I was a respected professional and academic.

When I had confirmation that Grace had been abused by Mark, she had been twice to the Amelia Child Bereavement service for play therapy with Brian. Grace was one of their youngest clients and I was advised that there would be limited benefit in her receiving this kind of support. I was determined that I would do everything I could to restore my child. I wanted to make it better. What else was I to do? So from the outset I had to argue that I needed the support for Grace and that she was mature for her four years.

Grace enjoyed her sessions with Brian, who was fun and encouraged her to talk about Daddy and her family, while they did fun things like making a memorial stepping stone and decorating a photo frame. He knew the complex circumstances surrounding Mark's death, but she had not demonstrated any cause for concern, expressing only a child's unconditional and naive love for her parent and trying to make sense of the sadness she felt. Grace was not withdrawn nor did she shy away from being alone with Brian. These sessions were fun and afterwards she could have time with Mummy on her own before we collected Joseph.

Returning for our third visit, I asked Brian if we could talk before Grace's session. She played happily with puzzles and colouring in the bright and comfortable waiting room under the watchful eye of the reception staff. If Brian was thrown when I told him about this new turn of events, he did not show it. But although he was empathic, he emphasised that his role, and the role of the Amelia centre, was not in abuse work, only in bereavement.

I felt desperate. From my training, I knew a little about child bereavement and abuse assessment and therapy, but nothing had prepared me to support my child who had been abused. Furthermore, the little I had been taught about the psychological aftermath of the abused child from my medical education was not good. Textbook and tutorials determined that the destiny of the abused child was a broken future. I felt helpless. I was terrified I might get it wrong, and confirm all that I had been taught.

This fear remains with me even today, despite considerable practice in the role; I now accept this anxiety of not being good enough or getting it horribly wrong will never go away. I remain frustrated by the numerous services we attended, all of whom at some point stated that they cannot address the grief and the abuse: just one or the other. Sadly, I have wanted to scream at all of them: 'But they are happening in one child – and that child and her mother have to cope with them all mixed up together! I can't split Grace down the middle or tell her today we do grief . . . tomorrow we'll talk about what happened with Daddy before he died.' It just doesn't work that way.

The notion that Grace was a closed book, perhaps in turmoil on the inside, haunted me. I am not sure, on reflection, if my desperation to help Grace talk about what had happened was driven more by my need to know or Grace's own needs. We seemed to be in no man's land.

CHAPTER 12

Into the Wilderness

Parents of young children can probably recall conversations where they were not really sure what their child was referring to. Little children seem to have a prolific memory for detail. Their rapidly developing brains store away so much from their few short years. One weekend, a few months after Mark's death, we were driving to a session with my friend Sky, a music therapist, when Grace stunned me from the back seat: 'Do you think the man from Washington will come back again?'

'What man from Washington! Who do you mean Grace?'

'The man from Washington like on the dollar. The man on the dollar came to see us.'

'Grace, I don't know anyone from Washington.'

'No you weren't there.'

I tried to ask more, my brain on alert again.

'No, Mummy. Daddy showed me, he was on the dollar bill.' It

made little sense but it unnerved me. Those words 'other boys' reverberated around in my thoughts once again. Suddenly, I was thrown into yet another reality. Her words confirming what until now had only been a terrifying thought, not fact. Could Grace have been subjected to abuse not just by her father but others, including a man from Washington? My imagination went wild with thoughts of groups of men in our home. My daughter sold for their titillation. And yet, when I allow myself to think of the photos taken, out there in the ether of the internet for the grabbing, that is exactly what was happening; perhaps even now, if only 'virtually'. If Grace was keeping this secret, how deep had she buried it? How terrifying could this have been or was this too sold as fun: a party with grown-ups?

As soon as I could I called Inspector Hutton and explained my worst fears. While Mark's criminal case was closed, the emerging details changed things but he was unsure how to proceed with such limited information, especially when Mark was not around to interview or to prosecute. Data from Mark's computer had led to a number of arrests and now the inspector told me that one such arrest was a man who lived in Washington DC. His phone number was found on a note on Mark's desk during the house search.

It is rare that when prosecuting internet-based perpetrators that an inspector has the opportunity to find and meet a child who is the subject of the images found. Grace's testimony could potentially provide concrete evidence, helpful in prosecuting those who have viewed her photos and who, in their defence, might try to claim this was a virtual child. But the main purpose of an interview would be to establish if other men were physically involved.

Grace was now recognised as a witness and a victim of crime. If they were going to take this further, then she would need to have a forensic physical examination and interview. It would be a challenge to get Grace to disclose even the abuse by her father to a stranger and, more difficult still, it was really the abuse by a stranger that they wanted to get to. The worrying part was that she was so young, and her bereavement so recent. Inspector Hutton and the investigation unit seemed uncertain what lengths they should go to in order to establish concrete evidence; they were weighing up the cost to all involved and the chance that anything meaningful would come from robust inquiry.

It was proving difficult to find an appropriate venue for her interview and a time when a police inspector could attend. Again, I felt desperate to know the whole truth and by this time part of me could still only believe the worst. The wait was intolerable.

With numerous delays, I had a sense that the authorities were sceptical. They did not seem to share my hunger to know the truth; the process of moving to the next level of investigation was slow and hesitant. Was I misinterpreting the signals? At the end of the day their job with thinly spread resources was to investigate crime, not support its victims. I would discover that you had to use your own initiative and go elsewhere for that.

And so my support did not come from the police. Clare had become increasingly concerned with the latest developments and contacted an old friend, John, from medical school who worked at the children's hospital in emergency medicine. She knew he was involved in examining children who had been abused. John put me in touch with the clinical lead, based at the hospital, who ran an outpatient clinic for children who had been abused. Although Grace did not meet the criteria to be seen in the clinic yet, as her case remained without proof from the authorities, Louise took time to meet with me and listen to our story. She found my concerns credible. From her expertise in caring for the abused child, she emphasised that children rarely make this stuff up and need to be believed. Louise encouraged me to trust my instincts; I was not just a paranoid mother.

I was so desperate for information. Although this was one of the most difficult conversations I had around that time, I came away with a much better understanding of the behaviour of those who sexually exploit children. I could piece together the signs that Mark had a serious addiction and forgive myself a little bit for missing them. Louise understood my feelings of inadequacy and guilt at having been so utterly deceived. She shared her own testimony of being physically attacked on a university campus. She understood my self-reproachful questions: how was I, an intelligent woman, so artfully betrayed? In my mind, this didn't happen to families like ours.

As I put events under the microscope, I could see how I had ignored my own instincts that something was wrong in our marriage. We spent three hours examining my life with Mark. I saw for the first time how the early years of doubt, and questioning if I loved Mark enough to marry him, had already put me on the metaphorical back foot: I had invested so much of myself in making our marriage work. Mark and I were so different, and how we were different confirmed to Louise that Mark had demonstrated some of the hallmarks of a man who was an endogenous paedophile. His sparse home, a virtually empty dwelling where he gave greatest importance to computers. Although outwardly vivacious and funny, inside Mark was a man who lacked any self-belief. Once we were married and I had established myself as a university professor, Mark's feelings of inadequacy had intensified. His own credentials, especially when measured side by side with his wife, left him feeling less of a man.

One Christmas, at an opulent department party at the museum of fine art, I listened incredulous as I overheard Mark telling other guests of his recent graduation from the MBA programme. He was yet to complete his undergraduate degree and, uncomfortably, I realised his embarrassment at what he thought of as his meagre academic achievement. I could understand his motivation for lying to save face; nevertheless, I felt sad that he felt he needed to do this. Little did I know then that his capacity to build a web of deceit stretched far beyond what could reasonably be imagined. Perhaps, surface dishonesty provided cover for the darkness of the deceit beyond it.

Louise could see how my work had drawn me away from Mark and provided me with a way of making meaning out of what life had become. Early in our marriage, Mark and I would bookend each day with a long commute in opposite directions. The day started at 5 a.m. and ended as darkness descended on the late evening. Every third night, I was required to be resident and on duty in the hospital. The demands of the hospital training were great and compounded by my flailing attempts to adjust to the newness of everything. I desperately wanted to return home to all that was familiar. Mark felt rejected: 'Am I not enough to make you happy?' He wasn't; I needed work to be the thing that grounded me.

Louise asked more about how I had struggled with these difficult transitions: I felt alien to the apparent enormity of American medicine and to the newness of married life. Although I had become a quietly confident and capable young doctor since medical school, my first year in America seemed to erode this. A seam of discontent ran through me that Mark could not reconcile. There was so little time for respite or to build our relationship. My holiday allowance was limited to just two weeks a year and the rota was gruelling, frequently exceeding 120 hours a week. I often came home utterly exhausted. Mark retreated to his office, perplexed by the complex emotional needs of his wife. My comfort was found in helping the patients I met and inadvertently this would become the object of my passion.

One case in particular was the trigger. Near the end of my first year training in the USA, I met Samuel, a patient whose experience drew me into a very emotional and time-intense area of medicine. I threw my heart and soul into my work and took another step away from Mark. Samuel had suffered a devastating stroke during a routine surgery. When we met, he had been hospitalised for over two years and was holding on to his life by a thread. He was an empty shell. His body was road mapped with tubing into every site feasible. Family rarely visited him and there were no photographs or stories to build a picture of who he had been before the operation. Samuel tried to die at least once a fortnight: his heart would stop. The surgeon in charge of his care would instruct us, his trainees, in bringing Samuel back from the brink. I began to question, 'Why?' What were we bringing Samuel back to? Why were we trying to defy his death?

Each day, as I attended to Samuel's failing health, I was struck by his suffering. It seemed intolerable. Our lives were fast paced and dynamic; Samuel's had barely turned a page in two years. His days were only punctuated by his limping from one crisis point to another. I could not stand by and allow this intolerable suffering to happen to another human being without questioning and calling us, as Samuel's caregivers, to account.

It was clear I had stepped out of line; to challenge senior clinicians was unheard of. News of my showdown with this most highly-respected surgeon spread through the hospital; I was advised to keep my head low for a while. The following week, I applied to train as a specialist in caring for the dying, a new field of medicine for America: palliative care. I chose to swim upstream against the tide, to be diverted by the challenge of a 'cause'. I had a new focus to feel passionate about.

As I described my career and my building awareness of how different we were as husband and wife, Louise helped me see that I could not balance the demands such a foreign existence had put on me and how, as we both struggled with the differences we found in each other living together for the first time, we became increasingly distant.

The distractions of full-time working in a demanding role also lent itself to exploitation. Mark was lone parent while I was working late or on call for the weekend. There were many times when I had no choice but to put my patients' lives and comfort before my family. As a doctor, I could not just walk out at the 5 p.m. bell. I had no other option but to trust and believe in his devotion to our children.

Louise helped me interpret Mark's behaviour. I was able to painfully recall how frequently, when I descended into the basement to say goodnight to Mark, the screensaver would abruptly black out the page he was working on. Exhausted by the ardour of the day or distracted by a need to internally debrief a challenging case, I remained without suspicion. As my refuge and strength grew at work, so Mark's own nemesis took a greater hold on his weaknesses and insecurity.

An essential credential in my work is empathy and the ability to facilitate this concept in others. It is therefore a paradox that my greatest misgiving and battleground with Mark was his apparent lack of empathy. Literature had taught me a lot about human suffering. I love books; stories with a social conscience or a human narrative hold the greatest appeal. They make me cry. Mark could not understand why I was moved to tears by these stories of people 'I didn't even know'. We spoke different languages when it came to our emotions. What was emerging was not a lack of social conscience but a void of empathic know-how. Frustration and despair intensified: Why can't I teach him how to feel?

Louise described how compassion and empathy require us to sacrifice something of ourselves to another person. Mark seemed to have had built such fierce defences that did not allow this level of vulnerability even with his wife. Louise wondered if he found my emotional unguardedness both terrifying and disabling. Mark responded to the factual content of our conversations – he could present such razor-sharp rational argument that those who encountered it found unnerving. But he lacked the emotional dexterity to respond to my feelings. He would ask me to give him a script: 'Tell me what you want me to say, just give me the cue and I will repeat it when you tell me to.'

There were often intense arguments, as neither of us could see things from the other's perspective. I would feel so trapped that sometimes I came close to leaping out of a moving car; I had the door open on the freeway, I was so desperate to escape his tirade of analytical thought. But we had overcome so many hurdles and created a costly existence, and so each time we fought I convinced myself that we had invested too much in our relationship, and we had travelled too far together, to just walk away. I buried my uncertainties. Louise showed me how this left me vulnerable to being groomed. I was in a perpetual state of convincing myself everything was OK.

Self-denial is my deepest regret. In that consultation, I came to understand how you can think you know someone but in reality you only see the version of themselves they want you to see. The abuser becomes a master of deception. When someone sets out to deceive the odds are stacked in their favour, especially if the other person has very emotionally driven reasons to believe. Until then I had not seen Mark as a skilled groomer and myself as an object to be groomed. I had only thought of Grace as being subject to mind games; now I could see how I too fell victim to this.

Denial, even in the aftermath when the evidence was emerging, was a valuable means of survival. I desperately wanted to hold on to any hope and to the better versions of who we believed Daddy to be. I wanted to believe that Mark was incapable of such crimes, both for me and for our children.

I needed to believe the best in others, especially those I loved. It was a principle that I lived by.

When I was training, I made a blundering error in trying to bring a patient's thinking back from what seemed quite plainly to me was a fantasy world. This woman had widespread cancer and for the professionals around her it was painfully obvious she only had a few weeks to live. Her denial of the painful truth was rigorous and my reality check was met with a raft of hatred; the therapeutic relationship was destroyed in an instant.

Rigorous denial: Had this been me? Had it been easier to accept this version of the truth about Mark, our relationship and our family? So much was at stake if I thought otherwise, and held up any reservations or suspicions for full and diligent scrutiny. Perhaps friends and family with their own objectivity could plainly see what I could not.

As Louise described the artful skill of those who abuse, I was to see clearly for the first time that part of Mark's grooming process for me was to subtly erode my confidence as a parent and a wife. He had played to my own insecurities about my body during and after pregnancy and my failed duties as a wife. During an argument, if I suggested we should separate I was threatened with the loss of my children. I wasn't sure if we could ever be happy. I had longed to move back to England at this point; life had begun to feel so treacherous.

Mark had understood all that we had put into our marriage, we had quite literally moved continents for each other, and he knew how much loss I would be inviting into our world if I chose to leave. He had recognised perhaps that I felt vulnerable as the foreigner with a limited understanding of the American child custody system. And our cross-cultural relationship had from the start been built upon a higher level of dependence on the person with insecurities of being far from home.

Furthermore, I had not considered the effort Mark had put in to maintaining his charade. Louise's experiences had taught her that Mark's efforts at deception were very purposeful. Once again I was at a disadvantage; I am not naturally suspicious and in fact I was relatively naive to this dark world of child sexual exploitation. I had not considered my husband to be a threat. Just like the majority of the general public, I had feared the paedophile stranger, the man on the news; not the man we loved. Louise asked me to forgive myself; far more attention has been given to teaching us about 'stranger danger', rather than the statistic that 90 per cent of sexually abused children already knew their perpetrator. Despite my training in assessing children who have been abused, I presented a relatively easy target for Mark's efforts to intentionally deceive. Exhausted by the effort of just getting through each day, I easily accepted his explanations for any inconsistencies. He had a naturally questioning and inquiring mind; I did not. I left my analytical 'know-how' behind at work. If I did question, he had already thought through a persuasive and forceful argument or answer in response. He was not working; he had time to plan and execute the unthinkable. Mark understood how I could easily get lost in my emotional response to a situation. He could help me to lose faith in my own judgement while he remained unshakeably cool and collected.

After Mark died, the clues emerged in piecemeal. The unfamiliar dirty child's blanket and the grubby baseball hat we had found in Mark's mangled trunk pointed to a man I did not know: another life. I had thrown them away in an instant, shoving them deep down into a black trash bag along with the sexy undergarments he had bought for me through the years of our marriage.

Mark's approach to gaining Grace's unquestioning trust was textbook. Grace loved to dance and sing. She loved to dress up and entertain us with one of her many shows. She seemed happy and her behaviour did not stretch beyond that of an ordinary four-year-old girl. She loved to spend time with both of us, equally. If Mummy was working for the weekend at the hospital, she settled happily for time with Daddy; indeed Daddy was fun. Mark was better at throwing himself through the obstacles of the local soft play, far more likely to share a pizza and not insist this was counter-balanced with a plate of fruit. He got excited by the idea of buying a bumper pack of crayons with which to colour large shared projects with Grace; as long as Grace coloured within the lines. Mark appreciated the thrill of a flume or a fast ride.

At the time, there were no alarm bells resounding in my soul. But as I talked, red flags appeared that I had not placed in their true context before. When washing Grace, I noticed that her vulva was very red and inflamed. In itself this is not so unusual; little girls do not have the patience or skill to wipe properly after toileting. Until now, this had seemed a perfectly rational explanation. My skin crawled as I thought of the wretched irony that, in caring for this problem and as part of teaching Grace about her body, I had emphasised that the application of cream to this area and touching her bottom should only be done by Mummy, Daddy, or a doctor with Mummy's permission.

I listened to Louise with horror. Children who have been groomed to accept sexual abuse may also demonstrate sexualised behaviours. I already knew this from textbooks and lectures. Until now I had dismissed Grace's flamboyant dancing as nothing more than a child mimicking the actions of trained dancers on the TV; none of this had struck me as hypersexual. Without a darker context, this had not seemed something more to worry about.

Mark had convinced Grace that sharing their secret was very special. Daddy had told her that Mummy had a lot of worries: a new baby, a sick daddy and lots to do at work. She did not want to upset Mummy. Louise could see, from the child's perspective, how very confused Grace was by the new things Daddy had shown her.

'Alice I can see that Grace was looking for reassurance. She was testing out Daddy's warning. It was early days, she was not yet satisfied by Daddy's explanation of the pictures she had seen in his computer. Perhaps Mummy would not be as upset as Daddy had said, and so she took a risk and cautiously broke a promise to Daddy, not to tell.' Louise paused. 'I can see how hard this is Alice. You were driving the car when Grace threw out her question, as a statement of fact: Did Mummy know that children sometimes drink from men's bottoms? Immediately, Mummy seemed shocked and Grace did not dare bring it up again. She could see it had not pleased her; just as Daddy had said it wouldn't.' Louise reached forward. 'It wasn't your fault, you didn't know. Mark had the upper hand;

he had prepared Grace for that reaction.'

Louise could see that I can't help but feel devastated; that one moment could have been a turning point. Instead twelve more months of intensive grooming followed and the door to Grace's world of abuse closed.

Mark's feelings of inadequacy and his internal struggles fuelled his interest in children. It was with children he could feel most comfortable. Louise, and the experts I have met since, suggest that for the paedophile gratification comes from the power imbalance they can experience in the relationship with a child. And just like Mark, a young child will function in a world of black and white; they do not yet have the emotional maturity to understand nuance or empathy. For me it is a poignant irony that the only book Mark read from cover to cover was Nabokov's Lolita: the story of an ardent paedophile and his stepdaughter, Lolita. I love the poetry of Nabokov's writing but find myself repulsed by the actions of his character, Humbert, who is obsessed with a twelve-year-old child. But what was Mark's fascination with this story – validation?

Our understanding of how and why someone becomes sexually attracted to children in a world so engaged with the internet remains inadequate. As my understanding of this predilection magnified, it was challenging to consider that perhaps Mark was also groomed by those he took shelter with. Forums help to mould those who access and supply child abuse images on the internet. They act as a support group, helping the abuser feel legitimate in their actions, normalising what they do. Mark was encouraged to take more risks and his role in the organisation of the forum was rewarded. He was a part of something; he was valued for his ability to organise, conceal and execute. It was these traits that had so successfully kept me in the dark; the qualities of a successful trader in images of child abuse. The perpetrator Louise knew only too well.

Just three hours with this skilled counsellor empowered me to trust my instincts, painful though they were. A clearer picture of what Mark had become and what had happened to us as a family was now emerging. I can only imagine just how overwhelming it would have been to be faced with the full reality in just one sitting on 25 July 2007. In retrospect, the piecemeal nature in which I learnt the reality felt a blessing: a gift of grace and kindness to my sensibilities.

Dancing around the truth became increasingly difficult at work. My colleagues supported me so well in the circumstances. They had already recognised the toll working in palliative medicine might take when I had just lost my husband. They donated their leave so that I could have longer off and I had taken on a reduced role – there was plenty of academic work to be getting on with, and teaching. Above all they wanted to help and knew getting back to work gave me some sense of being grounded again. It was vitally important to all of us what we did. But despite this, I was finding it increasingly difficult to balance my emotions at work. I was broken, distracted by the new threats that were emerging and in a state of suspense, waiting for a plan. To create flexibility in my schedule, I decided I needed to tell more of my work colleagues, so told two close colleagues and our division director.

The morning of Grace's appointment for a forensic physical

examination, I shifted my work around and literally prayed that no one would page me. The clinic was just one block away from the main hospital and I hoped no one would see us going in. I existed in a world of palpable shame; a pervading sense that I was stained by Mark's actions.

I was advised to keep things very simple and straightforward when I explained to Grace why we were going to the clinic. I should not fill her head with any leading thoughts about what had happened. I should tell her that a doctor was going to examine her and that this was a place where children were seen who had experienced similar things to Grace; the things she had told me had happened with her daddy. As we walked to the clinic from the parking lot, we passed a colourful playground; I promised Grace she could play there when we came back out.

I felt sick with anxiety. I hated that my daughter was having to go through this and feared how she might respond. Grace was nervous but also curious. A sweet drink and snack while we waited helped her to settle in. I went into a separate room to provide some history to the doctor, and Grace was shown a treasure chest of toys where she could pick something out to take home later.

The examination did not take very long, but I was horrified as my tiny little girl sat in the clinical chair with her legs in the gynaecological stirrups. This had always seemed barbaric, even for an adult: so exposed. And then a larger than life camera took zoom photographs of her genitals. Grace really took all of this in her stride. Unlike me, she was not obviously disturbed by the camera directed at her. Perhaps by this time Grace was so desensitised to having photos like this taken.

Mark had taken many, perhaps with onlookers, and horrific though it might sound: this was not a lot different.

The examination concluded that there had been no penetrative trauma. That evening it struck me, did they not find Grace's calm acceptance of the whole process pathologic? Surely a child of Grace's age would normally resist such attention?

Grace ironically came home with a dollar store version of an over-sexualised Bratz doll from the treasure box, which broke within a day – thank goodness. The rag doll from the Amelia Centre, who we affectionately named Sky, lives on and until very recently shared a place with other preferred soft toys on Grace's bed. I am sure there is some irony and blessing in this: I didn't want Grace to remember the forensic clinic experience.

Talking about what had happened proved a lot more challenging. There were no words to be found. A common language had not been provided for her experience; Mark had groomed this out of our usually chatty girl.

Initially, there was a lot of red tape about where the interviews would happen; a suitable unit could not be located. Every day I remained on tenterhooks as the police and the child protection services debated amongst themselves where best to interview Grace. The abuse service was overwhelmed, as was police time. Grace would need to be interviewed in one of their video-linked clinical interview rooms. A police presence ordinarily was needed, in order to guide any questioning, particularly if information emerged that might lead to prosecution. The area that the local authorities covered was expansive and at one point an appointment was set which involved us travelling nearly 200 miles away for the interview.

How would I convince Grace to come on this day out?
Eventually, after further discussion about Grace's age and the
likelihood that she would disclose, it was decided that we
would be interviewed in our own city and the police would not
need to be present: videotaped recording of the sessions would
suffice. One morning, to everyone's surprise, an appointment
was offered locally just three miles from our home.

This office was in one of the poorest and most run down
parts of the city. It was an area that locals avoided unless they
lived there. It was part of my nightmare that we found
ourselves driving into this parking lot and sitting in the
waiting room. As we parked, I imagined that my shiny
hubcaps might be one of the costs of this experience. I found
myself questioning, Why am I here? Our family doesn't fit here.
This shouldn't happen to doctors and their families, surely?

I don't think it was about snobbery. More that it was all just so
incongruous to me. But child sexual abuse is not loyal to a
particular demographic group; it does not have a predilection for
the socially deprived or financially impoverished. It cuts across
society lines and lies hidden in many different kinds of family.

On route to our first forensic interview we passed a car
accident. Grace was clearly affected by seeing this accident, as
was I. We found ourselves being diverted across the road from
a mangled piece of black metal not dissimilar to Mark's own
car. We said very little. I was trying to prepare Grace for what
was to come, but it was not going well. She didn't want to talk
to anyone else, just Mummy. She had not wanted to leave her
friends and the fun of pre-school that afternoon.

The waiting room was a shabby, sticky-carpeted room. On
an unloved wooden shelf were a few broken toys with missing

parts: a farm without any animals, puzzles without all their pieces, and colouring pens that had run out of colour. For four weeks, Grace was bribed with sticky rice crispy bars and sweet drinks. How I hate rice crispy treats; our feet stuck to that carpet because of them. No other clients arrived while we were there – for this, I was grateful. At that initial meeting, the interviewer remained on a chair seated a little distance from Grace. I was struck that she never joined Grace on the carpet or engaged in play right there in that room. It did not feel like she made a great attempt to put Grace at her ease.

For three further weeks, Grace would not move from the floor of the waiting room. We tried some middle ground: the interviewer's office. This was a small cluttered room with little space for her clients. Yet, Grace seemed more comfortable within its confines; a doll's house provided an escape, as the grown-ups spoke. But we were only allowed to remain in this room for a short time; it was not somewhere to get comfortable as Grace needed to move to the video-link room. Time was beginning to run out, we would soon be leaving for England.

Preparing for each of our visits, I tried hard to explain that it was really important she talk to someone else other than Mummy. As the weeks passed and we were making no progress, I was advised it was OK to talk about what Daddy had done because these interviews were not about that and they were not therapy either. It was so hard not to ask leading questions. It was very difficult to separate the 'daddy' from the actions he took. I was well aware that I did not want to demonise my children's father, but I was also concerned that I was battling with Mark's own rationale, which had of course become ingrained in Grace's: 'what happened was alright because it makes boys feel happy'. I needed her to understand that Mark's actions were wrong and that he made some very bad choices, as grown-ups sometimes do. I was also worried that we would create even greater confusion in her mind and that potentially Grace would feel an even greater loyalty to preserving the secrets they had shared.

The interview room with its stark-white walls and little decoration, had indiscreet cameras mounted in each corner of the room. The interviews would be videoed and a police officer would watch them at a later date. They might be used in court. There was a low white melamine table with two chairs; some paper and crayons sat neatly on the table. A couple of rag dolls lay in another deep wire basket. I recognised these dollies from my training: shabby clothes which covered anatomically correct body parts. Nothing about this area or its contents enticed a child inside. It was clinical and cold.

Time was running out, we had a flight booked for England in a matter of weeks. I became increasingly desperate for Grace to go into this room. She had begun to dread our appointments and each visit was beset with tantrums about leaving nursery to go there. Why should she leave this place of fun and friendship to enter this uninviting place? It was important to question who or what I was doing this for: Grace, justice or my own need to know?

Finally, almost a month of weekly visits had passed. We agreed to a fourth and final attempt and Grace conceded to a few minutes with the interviewer if Mummy could come with her. They were happy that this was enough to provide me with reassurance; although it would not provide legally rigorous evidence. We went hand in hand along the corridor to the interview room. In the hallway Grace was once again offered a gift from a large basket of toys; we knew the routine by now: somehow a gift might make it all better. Despite the bribe Grace took a lot of coaxing to say anything at all.

The interviewer showed Grace some pictures, illustrating good touch, which slowly transitioned to areas of bad touch. Grace was encouraged to say who did what to her: who gives you hugs, Grace? Who kisses you on the mouth? Who can touch you there, Grace? She was bravely able to clearly indicate that Daddy had touched her, but denied that anyone else had done so. Grace showed no emotion or distress in this dialogue only detachment and a reluctance to tell.

The investigators were happy to believe that Mark was the only perpetrator. I wanted to believe it too. I wanted to feel relief, but I couldn't. By now I had become conditioned to expecting the worst and to remain suspicious, even when reassured otherwise by professionals. I am not sure if I will ever know the whole truth. I was somewhat relieved that we had finished this process, but sadly unsure that any good had come from it. I felt guilty that I had felt so driven to put Grace through these interviews in my desperate need for the truth, but I don't think there has been any lasting harm. Thankfully, I think these sessions are more firmly engraved in my own memory than Grace's.

CHAPTER 13

Selling Up and Departure

It never crossed my mind not to move back to England. I had been wishing for this return home since my father had been diagnosed with cancer the previous year. It had been painfully traumatic to cope with the death of one parent while in the US. And emotionally, losing my dad catapulted me into the reality that I might face the same fate with my mum. I knew I could not repeat the experience at such a distance. The irrational belief that more people you love will be taken from you torments the bereaved.

Looking back, our move across continents and the systematic dissolution of a ten-year relationship happened very quickly. I sometimes wonder if I had this to 'do over' would I do it differently. Would the funeral happen at a decent interval from Mark's death? Would I halt to contemplate before dropping off all of Mark's clothes, books and belongings at the thrift store? Would I have waited a year before moving house? Moving continent? Bereavement experts certainly recommend no haste in these tasks: no, indulge your grief and take things slowly. In her book Tear Soup, Pat Schwiebert describes how a ponderously stewed 'grief soup' is placed on a low flame and may simmer for as long as needed. But I was on a rapid conveyer belt of despair, indeed my feverish stew was on a rapid boil. In just three months, what remained of ten years of my life was packed into three small memory boxes: one for each of us left behind. Clothes, books, bikes and a treadmill were packed into a shipping container. And a home was liquidated in a weekend garage sale.

Selling what amounted to almost the entire contents of a home is a strange affair. It is quite one thing to have an estate sale for someone you have loved who has died. And certainly, I do not underestimate the emotional burden of this. But, I would say it is almost farcical to observe your own 'estate sale' while you are still very much alive. We created a long inventory of items to ship, sell, donate or dump, and sale items were given labels. Our garage took on the appearance of a pioneer store worthy of the early settlers. And then I watched as, from dawn to dusk, a crowd of acquaintances and strangers trailed through our house, bargaining even for the half-used cereal packets in our pantry, sometimes with very little sensitivity.

The memories flooded out of the door. Much of our furniture would look out of place in an English home; it was too large and furthermore would be too expensive to ship and store until we found somewhere new to settle down. The furniture we could barely afford as newlyweds was sold for a fraction of its worth. We had struggled to furnish our first home together on our meagre earnings; our bank account had barely stretched to cover a mortgage and my immigration costs. The dining room had remained empty for many months. A pine table which had eventually graced this space was bartered over and finally sold for a song. Although I was present for the sale, on hand for any questions, I functioned as a bystander. Close friends who had experience in estate sales thankfully handled the money. At the end of a long two days, the sale could be declared a success and what little remained was left out for the final thrift store donation.

As my home stood empty and I prepared for our final week, staying at a friend's home, Mark's aunt and cousins arrived to say their farewells. I had not seen them since his funeral three months earlier. It was an unusual meeting in our front room with only one chair and three guests, but I tried to play hostess. It was touching that they had made a four-hour drive for such a limited exchange. Everything about that meeting felt uncomfortable and awkward. Their sentiment was genuine, and yet it seemed strange because they knew so very little of what had passed beyond how Mark had died. I held back from telling even a little of the truth.

There was no time to dwell on what had just passed. There was still so much to do in those remaining days. I was surviving. The land was barren.

Somehow, work remained a part of life's rich tapestry in these frantic days. I prepared transcripts for lectures, taught communication skills to our trainees, organised our quarterly bereavement service and I now had resumed some very limited clinical duties. The first of these, certifying a dead body, had seemed on the outside a fairly neutral task, after all, years of medical practice desensitises us to such experiences. But I would look into the eyes of the young and the old who had died and my mind would drift to thoughts of Mark's corpse: just as cold and lifeless. I would question again if I should have asked to see Mark after he died, and my mind would again wonder what he might have looked like. Would his face and hands be scarred and distorted beyond recognition? Would I have wanted to shake him and shout at him? Again I would conclude that I may have come undone.

Worse still, my capacity for holding the loss of others in my hands was considerably reduced. The bread and butter of my job was talking to those whose loved ones were dying and helping them to navigate this no-man's land of emotional landmines. The work was intense and, while personally very gratifying, exhausting even to the robust in heart. Two losses in quick succession seemed set to rob me of the life's work that so fulfilled me.

In his study, When Bad Things Happen to Good People, Rabbi Harold Kushner describes his philosophy that the comfort provided to those in despair comes in the form of an army: an army of mortal angels, who gather around and lift up friends when they fall down. My professional family organised a wonderful leaving party. What I remember most about the occasion was the outpouring of love from those who really had been the closest thing to family for six years. They came to my rescue without question or curiosity. Only as we boarded the plane to England did Faye share with them the whole of our story; they have never demanded to know more from me.

At the leaving party, as I looked around in the late autumn sun, my eyes feasted on the army God had sent to my rescue; I was, and I remain, so very grateful to these amazing human beings. I was touched by the words of Jess, a friend who in a short speech commented that this outpouring reflected the kind of person I was. I needed those words of encouragement right then and I still do. I am OK. When I look back at the photographs of this event, I am struck by how tired and drawn I look and by how tiny Joseph was, just a baby, passed from arms to arms. I am OK.

One of my friends sacrificed more in this episode than any other. Even to this day, she bears considerable wounds from the path we travelled on together. I am eternally grateful to Clare, who became like a sister from the moment Mark disappeared. Saying goodbye was hard and somehow marked the end of something truly amazing. Just as the images of all that Mark had done plagued my mind, I believe they did hers. She was remarkable in her compassion towards me and yet, inside, I now realise she was burnt up with anger at Mark.

Only now do I perhaps also recognise Clare's frustration with my need to create a balance between the grief for a father and a husband who had died and the awfulness of his actions beforehand. She wasn't just angry with Mark; she was angry with me. In her eyes, I tolerated too much in him, and had not done everything to help Grace heal. When I finally mustered up the resources to return to America, three years after Mark had died, Clare tearfully shared with me her anger that I had shipped Grace's bed. Mark had bought Grace this bed as a surprise when we returned from my six-month sabbatical. The bed was every four-year-old's idea of the bed Sleeping Beauty might have laid on for her hundred-year sleep. A sturdy four-poster with glittery drapes, it dominated Grace's bedroom when fully adorned. I was sensitive to the idea that this might be one of the few lasting gifts from her father. To Clare, this bed was sordid. It was the crime scene and a provocateur of dark and horrific memories that might lie in the deepest recesses of my little girl's mind. The bed needed to be destroyed, not treasured, and should never have been shipped. The bed does remain. Its posts have been disassembled and the pink, sparkly chiffon curtains have been packed away. I have offered to Grace over the years, with each room renovation, a new bed; my offer to date has been declined.

The day before our final departure from the USA, I had my final meeting with Inspector Hutton. This time I took Jess with me, a trainee psychologist and friend, who also flew back to England with us for a week to help me travel and transition with the children. For the inspector, the purpose of this final meeting was for me to hand over some physical evidence he had requested. This would aid the prosecution of anyone who held images of Grace on their computer. The second objective was to see if I could identify the girl known as Lisa Marie in Mark's files. This was only our second meeting; our first since the files had been discovered on Mark's home computer.

Evidence had been set aside when I organised items for shipping and the estate sale, in particular I had to hide the Cinderella and Sleeping Beauty costumes Grace so loved. To this day, I have had to nonchalantly excuse their absence in our shipping to Grace. These pretty baby blue and pink satin dressing-up clothes were handed over so that they could be placed in a dusty box in a police vault. I wonder how many such boxes exist. The scanty adult underwear viewed in many of the photographs, which Inspector Hutton had also requested, had been hastily thrown into a black rubbish bag and put out with the more ordinary garbage weeks before. Throwing out this trash happened in a moment of anger, and with a need to distance myself from anything vaguely sexy in my previous life with Mark. While I was disappointed to have failed to produce further evidence against potential violators of my daughter's innocence, she had been wrapped and tied in these lewd articles of clothing; I was also relieved that these intimate remnants of a flawed marriage were not going into that vault.

There seemed little that was private about my life in the room where the meeting took place. In moments of despair, sitting at that dusty, grey boardroom table, I also imagined that the inspector and his team had viewed some more intimate images Mark had taken of me. I felt ashamed that I had reluctantly agreed to let him take these shots: to leave for him while we were apart for six months. He had appealed to me to recognise that men have certain sexual and physical needs. He made me feel like a prude in my reticence. And although I was never fully naked in these images, I might as well have been; my skin crawled with the embarrassment of such a possibility. Although I am sure they have seen a lot worse. Indeed, Grace had endured so much more.

The most emotionally laden piece of evidence I had been asked to gather was the solid, heavy, steel-headed handheld juicer. It resembled a Tudor instrument of torture or battle. Just the week before, I had ricocheted from the inspector's phone call to prepare for today's meeting and grabbed this from the collection of kitchen utensils laid out on the kitchen table to be shipped. I had placed it in the bag of satin and faux fur of the dressing-up clothes. I was tormented by Inspector Hutton's over-the-telephone description of how this had been used to lure Grace into an act of oral stimulation. The camera images told the story. Click, click, click . . . First, placing the hard-headed object in her mouth and then, worse still, resting its macerating point between her thighs. This tool of Mark's grooming weighed down the plastic bag and tore a hole in its side with its sharp point. It is hard to imagine how someone can see such a use for a kitchen utensil, which previously had just lain innocently among the more mundane wooden spoons, plastic measures and spatulas of our kitchen drawers. It had been rarely used for its purpose of squeezing juice from the flesh of citrus fruit. What kind of mind makes this leap? How can such a squalid plan be conceived? I find it hard to walk down a supermarket's utensil aisle now.

Inspector Hutton reassured me of the gains that had come from the evidence unveiled so far. Over 200 men were being investigated as a result of Mark's case. Several large forums dissolved, a main server in Texas storing a wealth of pornographic data had been shut down and he was certain that more arrests would follow. Although Mark had died, some good had come from all that had passed.

As if to comfort, he advised me that, if alive, Mark might have been facing up to twenty years in prison. Those who committed crimes against children are rarely tolerated by fellow inmates. Often tortured and abused by other criminals, they are outcasts even in the prison world. I recognised that Mark was weak and would not have survived his punishment. It was implied, and I dare to say it: Mark was probably better off dead.

And how would we have navigated the likely road of shame? It is not hard to imagine the complicated lives or emotions of children who might want to visit their father in prison. Our lives would undoubtedly have been very much more public if Mark were alive. The media spotlight may have fallen upon us. Its interest might have been fleeting, but the damage far reaching. No, without a doubt, we had been saved and for that I am grateful.

(What had Inspector Hutton advised Mark was going to happen next when he left that interview room? Was the evidence not conclusive enough at that stage to bring a conviction? I forgot to ask.)

Finally: our conversation came to Lisa Marie, whose images had been discovered among those of Grace and had been coded by Mark in the same way. She looks up at me from her picture, her knickers hanging lifelessly about her skinny ankles. She stands to the side of a trashy unmade bed, in a room with peeling and dated wallpaper. A discarded Walmart carrier bag lies on the grubby bed in the background. It is the kind of room you imagine can be hired by the hour. She is about eight years old. Her pelvic area has been concealed from our view on this day by a whiteout strip. This young girl seems like a shell of a child. Her face speaks of the ability to disassociate, a phenomena described in those who are subjected to repetitive trauma: the mind separates itself from the body and all it is experiencing. (Yet the memory still forms, buried in a physical language, such as a flinch to human touch or a cold sweat when walking through a hotel lobby.)

I did not recognise Lisa Marie, but to this day I am haunted by her image. I feel a tight armlet of guilt at the stark reality that I have not been able to save her. If I allow myself, I can still see her face and I wonder what her story was and where she is now. The truth is that most children who are subjects of pornography remain nameless; they have no identity. They disappear into the ether. No one knows who they are or where they have come from. And perhaps it is because they exist without a story that their perpetrators can justify to themselves that they are harming no one. In a sense, these children are 'virtual' by default.

Grace remains the rare exception to this anonymity rule, for I know her story and so do others. I sometimes imagine occasions when Mark might have crept out to meet Lisa Marie, in the sordid room that was in the photograph. I have even contemplated that he met her in those three brief hours that passed unaccounted for before he died: one more for the road. I am disturbed by the thought of that worn child's blanket in the boot of his car. It did not belong to us. And although I was never there, I have flashbacks to scenes; they are a product of this one photograph. In one of my later counselling sessions, I was encouraged by the therapist to allow my mind to develop these images to their worst possible scenario and to let them have life, so that in time I would be desensitised to them. In truth, my mind's eye sometimes takes me to a vulnerable place where my own child stands in a similar room, her knickers dropped to the floor and she too disassociates. No one would wish to go there.

Inspector Hutton wished us well and I thanked him for the work that he and his team do. He offered to update me should there be 'the need'; but he is a busy man and in subsequent attempts to contact him we missed one another all but once. I wonder how we might define 'the need'. It is hard to imagine a vocation much more heart wrenching than my own; on the precipice of what challenges us as human beings: death. But I wonder what it takes to be able to work in the field of sexual crimes against children and how they sleep at night. I imagine you have to be emotionally robust, switching off from the job on the drive home. Driven perhaps by justice, but to survive you would need very clear boundaries; an inspector could not feel a personal connection with the victims and their families. That many remain nameless must help. How do you sit and look at countless indecent images of the same child? Imagination would need to be suspended. My training and experience has taught me to how to hold the wasteland of human suffering at arm's length, but no amount of procedure and learning has made me invincible and some stories just stay with me. I am human after all. Inspector Jack Hutton left this department a year later. He has his own children.

CHAPTER 14

Building Another Continent

The roller coaster did not pull into the platform for some time to come. We landed, moved in with my mum, and our family drew in a long sigh of relief to have us safe within their fold.

I was twenty-eight pounds lighter and still struggling with my relationship with food. Exhausted, but tasked with building a new life for us, I kept myself very busy. Grace started school, and I balanced looking after Joseph with taking steps towards returning to work. Just two months passed, in which time: Joseph learnt to walk, I bought a new car, began working as a GP, and even started to contemplate buying and furnishing a house of our own. The practicalities of making a fresh start were the easy bit. Healing the wounds of a broken heart would take a lot longer.

In crossing the Atlantic, I encountered an entirely different attitude to what we needed as a family. In the USA, there had been no doubt that both Grace and I would need years of therapy, and that this needed to get started as soon as possible. I felt under a lot of pressure to get it 'right', and to ensure Grace did not develop mental health problems or socially misconstrued behaviours as she grew older. I was advised that, typically, girls who had been sexually abused and groomed to accept sexually explicit behaviour would often become precociously sexual, or that Grace may become promiscuous at a very early age if I did not reset her boundaries. As you might imagine, this would set the fear of God into any parent.

Paradoxically, in England, I encountered an ethos that was so polar opposite in thinking that I quickly became confused about what was for the best. Desperate not to create trauma, I chose to follow the advice that it was too early in Grace's development to introduce her to therapy. Instead, I was assured that Grace would do as well as I did. If I coped well and provided a happy, loving and secure environment, she would flourish, too. The bottom line everywhere I turned for advice was that I needed to be the one to help my children, and Grace especially, through this trauma. The weight of this responsibility felt enormous and overwhelming. I wanted someone else to help me make it all right again for Grace. Already, the task of being a single parent seemed all-consuming and this other layer added just another weight to the load.

My counsellor and friend, Faye, had been essential in those early days and, now settled in England, I knew if I were 'to be there' for the girls I needed to find someone to continue to help me with the cauldron of emotions still simmering just below the surface. The relationship with Faye had worked, despite our crossover of a working relationship; there was sufficient foundation in place even before Mark died. Finding her replacement proved more difficult than I had anticipated.

Christmas came and went in a blur that first year. Grace, thrown into a classroom of strangers, struggled to find her feet. To make things worse she had joined the class midway through the first term. My heart sank each time the teacher called me aside to tell me that Grace had become inconsolable in class or had been at the centre of a playground upset. My worst fears were played out as the teacher theorised – not knowing her history – that Grace liked to play the victim and consciously put herself in these situations. The teacher had just completed a short course on childhood losses and bereavement; she was recognised as the school's grief expert. Indeed, she was highly qualified, equipped with plenty of academic understanding for situations just like ours. A first year school report cut me to the core: 'Grace finds making friends challenging. She wants to be the centre of attention and becomes very demanding if she is not. Grace finds it hard to express her feelings appropriately, often becoming near hysterical over a very trivial matter.' There seemed to be a lot of theory but little understanding or empathy, between the words, for the trauma and loss my child had, and was still, experiencing.

At home, I would fall prey to the little knowledge I had of Grace's trauma. When our morning or evening routine became beset with tantrums over clothing, Grace would scream, dissolving into panic if clothing felt tight around her neck as she pulled a dress or sweater over her head. Then images of my child bound in adult lingerie and titillating costumes, as described by the inspector, overran my thoughts. It was impossible to not believe the worst. I began to perceive the moral imperative of finding help for Grace. I explored private support but ultimately went to our GP who referred us to the local Child and Adolescent Mental Health (CAMH) team.

I dared to believe I might, at last, find support in helping my children through this immense trauma. In error, I took Grace with me to our first and last appointment at CAMHs; they did not want to see her, just me. Once again, I told our story as Grace played in the waiting room under the watchful eyes of a stranger. Very quickly, I realised they were not interested in helping Grace. The threat had been removed; Mark was dead. The events had not happened in their locality and she was no longer at risk. It was their perception that Grace was too young to have any lasting memory of what had happened or, at the very least, she was unable to assign any significant meaning to her experience because she lacked any 'sexual' frame of reference.

It was their opinion that Grace would be unable to engage in therapy to either address her grief or abuse. They believed that what was needed was my discernment of the situation. I needed to be cognisant of interpreting normal child behaviour and separating it from symptoms or signs of abuse. The best they could offer was a parenting course, which would run the next summer. This would give me the skills to manage any difficult behaviour. I was given a book on child development to take away to get me started. Once again I was advised that

Grace's best support would come from me.

When the letter came to invite me on the parenting course I declined. I felt a little indignant that my parenting skills were in question. It was not my skills but the situation that were exceptional. On reflection, I am not sure if this was what was implied. By then, I was working as a GP in the area, and the parents of children I had referred for mental health support had also been referred to this course. It seemed to be the current band-aid for children in severe distress. But I could not have imagined sitting in a circle with other parents, sharing the details of our lives and retaining my professional boundaries. It simply would not work.

One of my greatest challenges has been resisting the urge to blame every meltdown on all that has happened. It is easy to catastrophise when you really have been through your worst nightmare and not just imagined it. Interpreting normal child behaviours and signs and differentiating these from symptoms of abuse is like trying to predict how a story might end when you have only read the first page. And, furthermore, it is pervaded by the fear of labelling your child, creating a victim and boxing her into behaving a particular way. I do not want to sell Grace short. I needed and still need to rebel against this.

Who would want to believe that this is their child's destiny? That she cannot escape a pattern of pathological behaviour and a certain emotional destiny. And yet I find myself thinking, Is this behaviour because she was abused? I had been taught that the abused child might have extremes of conflicting emotions which may manifest as volatile or clingy behaviour, or the very opposite, withdrawal and a flat, detached state of being. Difficulty at school, in relationships or a reluctance to engage with activities they previously enjoyed may all be part of the picture. In particular, I had learnt to be on the alert for any physical signs of abuse or overtly sexual behaviour; to be tuned into avoidance of particular adult company or talk of secrets. The lecturers take-home point is that the child who has been abused may seek out sexual relationships prematurely and become furtively promiscuous. They may break all the rules, and challenge boundaries or parental authority.

In the New Year, I began the search for a new counsellor to support me. I would follow the expert opinion and maximise my own emotional resources. I had good advice not to settle on the first therapist that I met. I needed to hunt around to find the right fit. I asked around for recommendations and several came highly recommended, but the experience of sharing my story and seeing how it was received was challenging, even among professional listeners.

The first counsellor did not feel equipped to handle my complex bereavement; the second wanted to cast Mark in the role of Satan at our first meeting and did not seem to recognise that I was not ready to hear this. I realised, it was one thing for me to feel angry with Mark but to hear someone else cast him down made me defensive and felt like a personal affront. It was complicated: I had loved this man, I was his widow and yet he had betrayed me in the most awful of ways. I understand why the battered wife defends her assailant; I understand Grace's naive defence of her father's actions in those early days. I wanted to hate him. Please don't get me wrong. But I didn't know how without also saying nine years of marriage had been a sham, that I was a fool and in essence blaming myself for choosing the wrong man. This snare remains an open trap, ready to grasp a vulnerable ankle and pull me down, even today.

It took two years and two very differently skilled counsellors to help me see that I was not to blame and that my complex feelings toward Mark, a mixture of love and hate, are entirely justified. I still struggle to hear others talk badly of him. I cope by distinguishing his horrendous actions from him, the man. People are not two-dimensional cards: bad or good. They are both bad and good and all that goes in-between. People are the product of their genes, their environment and all that life has thrown at them. And sometimes I can even forgive him.

The stumbling block for each of the counsellors I had met so far was the complexity of the sexual crime Mark had committed and its complex relationship with our already grieving family. I am not sure if I remember how I ended up approaching the Lifecentre for help but it was the best 'chance' I have taken to date. A Christian charity, the Lifecentre provides counselling for survivors of sexual abuse and rape, including those who have been abused and those who support them. Last year, they received over 14,000 calls for help in the form of telephone calls, texts and emails; this resulted in 400 face-to-face referrals and over 3,000 counselling sessions.

Making the first phone call felt shameful. Once again, I had to acknowledge the details and that our family had been affected by sexual abuse. In hushed tones and alone in the cold hallway of my old family home, my story unfolded into

the empty space. A few details were gathered and a letter
arrived a short while later, inviting me to an assessment
consultation. I would meet my counsellor at a safe house and
have an initial assessment to see if my case was appropriate
for support. As I'd found elsewhere, Grace was considered too
young to benefit from any formal therapy. They advised me
that it was unusual for them to counsel a parent of child
victim of abuse – already I felt different, but also accepted.

When I reimagine that initial session, I can remember the
lightness of the room and the apprehension I felt in telling my
story again. But by now the details were well rehearsed; telling
my story had become almost like reading a script. From here it
would take a skilled counsellor to unlock the emotion within,
to expose what felt like 'another life' and to help me to
connect.

By this time, I had been in 'survival mode' for so long I had
reached a point where I struggled to feel anything. I was so
confused by my emotions. I would feel fearful tension building
just beneath the surface but could not find a way to release it. I
had a much clearer idea of the circumstances surrounding
Mark's accident but felt so distant from the man I had
married; the man I thought I knew and loved. Tears would not
fall where or when they were needed.

I knew I had to summon the courage to open an envelope
Clare had given me a few days before we had left America.
This contained the photographs she had taken at the scene of
Mark's crash and of the car at the wrecker's yard. I wanted to
feel something other than just conflict; to feel something for
Mark, to connect with the grief, to love him and feel the loss
of a husband. Alone, I pulled these photos out of their clean

plain brown envelope and looked down on the images of burnt grass and debris but worse still of a car bent-double only on the driver's side, the seat blown to shreds and blood-stained remains of upholstery. I could feel something again. I could cry. This scene of human destruction brought the feeling back to the surface, in shattering waves from where they had been buried.

Gratefully, a few weeks later, I began my weekly sessions with Sara. I learned to create space around these sessions and to slide into the inconspicuous terraced house, hoping never to be recognised or to meet someone who might ask where I was going. Tension ebbed and flowed through my every pore as I walked up the street and stopped at the intercom to announce my arrival each week. Then a corridor of painted butterflies led me to the waiting room; they held the promising words: 'Just when the caterpillar thought the world was over, it became a butterfly.'

For a year, in those sessions, my story of a ten-year relationship unfolded and we thrashed out the questions that hung in the air: how did I marry someone who was so different from me? Mark was so death avoidant; I was so open to embracing my own and other's mortal wounds. Friends and family now feel able to say that they could not understand why I had married Mark. How could I have been so oblivious to what had been going on in my own home? Did I still love him? Why had I denied my gut feelings that something wasn't right? What will the future hold for my children, who will one day need to understand what had happened? How will they forge some kind of relationship with the man they called Daddy but scarcely will have known or remember? How will I carry the weight of being the person who holds for them the story of who Daddy was? There were so many questions. I don't think we found many absolute answers. What helped was to say out loud all that I feared and to acknowledge to someone else my own misgivings. Sara gave me the opportunity to grieve for my husband and all that we had lost.

Each session concluded in prayer, and as time passed I seemed to have cultivated a willingness to move forward. I had told and retold my story and as a result learnt to live alongside both the grief and the trauma. Each reading of the tale seemed to diminish its power over me. Sara accompanied me through that year of dreaded firsts: moving to a new home, Mark's birthday, our wedding anniversary, the children's birthdays, a holiday, and the first anniversary of the crash. Each was met with a feverish anxious prelude that would sometimes last weeks and intensify in the days just before the marked event. I learnt that the anticipation of each of these occasions was consistently worse than the day itself. There was an insatiable need to mark the date - to 'do something' – and then the days would just come and go like any other, with very nearly a sense of anti-climax. It is akin to the stew that some of us get ourselves into for Christmas each year. My sessions with Sara helped me to grieve all that I had lost and acknowledge the blessings as well. A year passed and I seemed ready to move on.

STEP FIVE Elephants Can Never Be Buried

Elephants are impossible to bury. In the wild, a family of elephants will desperately try to conceal their dead loved one with leaves and branches, ripping this shroud from neighbouring trees and brush, hoping to disguise the corpse from potential scavengers and predators. Overawed, I offered my elephant the same ritual covering. Conditions tore down this surface burial; it was never built to last.

Just as I thought I had laid open the meat of the matter and seemingly dissected the body of my elephant, menacing creatures intruded our sacred space: hyenas let out their piercing call to battle and vultures scattered pieces of the carcass in the blood-stained sand. From the impact of our fall, deep cracks had formed in the dry earth which spread like the fault lines of an earthquake into the surrounding landscape. My world felt treacherous and a dangerous place once more.

Tenacity is essential when faced with such beasts. It was only human to want to look away as they ripped at the carnage. Hyenas eat at night. Vultures swoop down in an instant. I had to hold on; to stare down these terrorists. It was important not to lose sight of how far I had come and not let them steal from me the significance of all I had digested so far.

What did I learn? Talk them down and they diminish, distancing themselves from the fabric of your being; vultures can become mere starlings in your soul.

CHAPTER 15

Driving, Flashbacks and Fear

Spring 2009

Two years on and life had become insanely busy. We had settled in a new home and Grace in her new school. I was trying to balance the demands of being a single mum and working part time, both as a GP and once a week as a specialist in palliative care at our local hospice. I had begun the process of duplicating my American qualifications in family medicine to establish myself back on the career path of the British medical system. It was easy at times to feel overwhelmed. It was then that the anxiety started.

At first, I noticed my breathing would change for days at a time. I had an insatiable need to yawn and fill my lungs with a deep breath. The tension in my chest would rise. This feeling seemed to come out of nowhere. It bothered me and I began to feel on edge. Only if I was completely distracted did this urge subside. I ruminated on these physical sensations, wondering why I felt this way and what I could do about it. Am I ill? Do I have uncontrolled asthma or, worse still, a serious illness like sarcoidosis or cancer? I knew this was a possibility. I met young women all the time in my job for whom this had become the reality, and they were dying. Fear escalated: I can't die. My children cannot become orphans. It did not make any sense because I could also have days on end of feeling absolutely fine. I even felt life had reached a new 'normal' that was pretty good.

I had made it through all those first year anniversaries and completed my course of counselling a year earlier. I had worked through some terrible questions that had hung like daggers in the air since the day life became less ordinary. I seemed to be in new territory. It was time for a fresh start. My grief seemed manageable. Although the waves of emotion felt intense at times, especially when they came out of the blue, the feelings were usually brief and certainly more sporadic.

In my floundering attempt to move on I felt it was time to meet other widows. I had a strong sense of feeling different and somehow lost when I met other mums in the park or at the school gates. They seemed so much more carefree. I found myself apologising and awkwardly mopping up their embarrassment when they simply enquired about my husband: did he mind moving to England? It was if I was asking them to hold my lead balloon. In my solitude, I felt I needed to find a group who would understand what it felt like to be on your own, and who shared an understanding of lost dreams. I planned to join a young widow's weekend away.

I went into the weekend full of hopeful expectation. If nothing else, it would afford me some space to feel and think for a weekend. I would be able to step aside from the treadmill of life and attend to my inner needs. Full of emotion, I began my first long distance drive alone since moving back to the UK. I was full of anxiety that morning. My head worried over how much to share. What will it be like to meet other widows? As I drove, my chest was tight and I felt very edgy.

Reaching the motorway, my mind wandered to thoughts of what it might have been like to drive into another car approaching from the opposite direction. It was not the first time I had thought about this. In fact, my mind has been drawn to this thought ever since the accident, and even now it occasionally creeps in. In my mind's eye, Mark's accident or sometimes even my 'imagined' own, plays out in pictures right up to the point of impact. As I passed a lorry I flinched, as the image of my car or Mark's hitting it straight on becomes so real. I hear the noise of metal upon metal and the loud crashing thud of the impact. I see a lifeless body thrown forward and a hopeless airbag deployed. I can see the smear of blood across the keys in the ignition. My thoughts and feelings are intense, although they may only last seconds. I am grabbed back from these ruminations by the thought of my children. How cruel it would be to lose a second parent this way. It wasn't that I felt suicidal. I somehow understood Mark's desperation. I felt both sad and frightened in these moments. Driving had never been something that had bothered me; I was a confident driver. But now that had changed and it made me feel vulnerable.

About two hours into my journey, the traffic slowed to a crawl as we passed a terrible accident pushed up against the central barrier. A car sat distorted, having skidded across the fast lane, penetrated the central barrier and halted upside down in the gravel on the opposite side. I imagined that the driver must have died. My imagination went no further. The pictures stopped and instead my body took over: hands shaking and heart racing, I willed myself to the nearest service station and ground to a stop. When I later arrived at the widow's retreat, I was still recoiling from this event. For me, tension was high.

Nothing prepared me for walking into a room filled with fifty young widows, all women bar one. None were over the age of fifty; many were in their thirties just like me. The intensity of emotion was palpable. We all had a story to tell. Never before, despite working in medicine, had I contemplated just how many young men die every year from illness. Many died before they reached a hospital; as a doctor or medical student I would never have met them or their families. I would only have heard of these phenomena in a lecture theatre: many of them sudden deaths.

After the initial introductions, we broke up into smaller more intimate groups to share with each other our own personal stories. I felt heavy with the uncertainty of how much to tell. It quickly became apparent to me how different my story was: I had survived a different kind of trauma. I was struck by how much love each of these women felt for their lost partner and, to some extent, how the memory of their relationships and the man they loved had become rose-tinted. I heard stories of bravery, of intimacy and of good men whose lives and marriages had ended too soon. Many had fought and lost a longer battle against the demon that is an incurable disease: cancer and cystic fibrosis, among others. A few had experienced a death that came out of nowhere, loss without warning: a sudden death – heart attack, a blood clot or a devastating seizure. Some of these men had died alone on a business trip, others lying in the bed next to their wife; for a few, desperate attempts at resuscitation had ensued on the bedroom floor. We all shared the burden of lost dreams and some of raising children without the other parent. Some found themselves suddenly very alone. We were all irreparably wounded; the anticipated direction of our lives changed forever. But I soon realised I had come looking for companionship in my dirty, messy story and that companion was not going to be found here.

The lowest point of the weekend for me was a candlelit memorial service, decorated by the delicate flame of tea lights, white linen drapes and accompanied by lilting song. The half-light lent itself to some cloistered tears and moments of quiet reflection. We were invited to bring photos and to write messages to our lost partner to place with a candle or pin up on a noticeboard. Connections might be forged with thoughts of the man we had lost and those who stood with us in our grief. But in that moment, I felt as alien to my feelings as I did to the other forty-nine widows. Sentimentality, warmth of feeling and love was not flowing through me: I discovered I was angry.

Anger has never been an easy emotion for me to express. It usually comes out all wrong. I am like a pressure cooker and I hold anger in until it somehow has to find its release. I had not really expressed anger towards Mark until this moment. In all my weeks of counselling sessions, I had not managed to get angry. It took listening to other widows to recognise it for what it was. I was angry that my story was not like the others, that my marriage felt like a farce next to these genuine unions. But perhaps in that moment, I was most angry that I had come seeking to feel connected and understood and instead I only felt more isolated and undone. Underneath all of these layers of regret, I was angry at Mark, I am sure.

Looking back, I can now appreciate the good that came out of that awful weekend. It gave me the kick I needed to feel even a little bit angry, and to direct that towards Mark and the world he was addicted to. No one else was or is to blame for how I feel. And if I was going to forgive, I had to get angry first.

It was in the wake of a weekend focused on grief that I truly understood that I was a survivor of trauma. I reread When Bad Things Happen to Good People as well as Surviving the Storms of Life and learnt that trauma comes in many guises. Most simply it can be defined as a deeply distressing or disturbing experience. The shoe fits here. Trauma can strike anyone; it shows no favouritism. It often comes out of nowhere, leaving the unexpected victim shocked by their assault, but its aftermath is often typified by some common threads. That the survivor of trauma feels that they may never 'get over it'. They are left feeling unsafe. I had a safe and rather naive childhood. I had never needed to contemplate the reality of the dark side of child abuse, paedophilia and pornography, except in a textbook or a classroom. I somehow felt impervious to this world. I believed that most people are good. Now, the way I viewed the world had been permanently shaken up and restoration seemed unlikely.

I did not consider myself to have post-traumatic stress disorder (PTSD) until the flashbacks started. I tried to ignore these feelings but they became more and more intrusive and disturbing. They seemed to be a disturbance of my imagination; they were the fears I felt unmentionable. The Mayo Clinic defines PTSD as:

... a mental health condition that's triggered by a terrifying event – either experiencing it or witnessing it. Symptoms may include flashbacks, nightmares and severe anxiety, as well as uncontrollable thoughts about the event.

Many people who go through traumatic events have difficulty adjusting and coping for a while, but they don't have PTSD – with time and good self-care, they usually get better. But if the symptoms get worse or last for months or even years and interfere with your functioning, you may have PTSD.

I had discovered that trauma feels overwhelming. Trauma is often unspeakable, and many are stunned into silence by its power over us. Trauma isolates, it makes us feel abnormal. We don't want anyone to see our brokenness. I put on my 'brave-save' face each day and lived life behind a mask. I often felt trapped in a web of false pretence or an avoidance of the truth. Trauma produces a state that is hyper-aroused. The traumatised brain defaults to alert systems that are hypersensitive and on the defensive. The traumatised re-experience the trauma over and over again. More frequent episodes of vividly reliving my own trauma were emerging. They became my unwelcome house guest. Nothing prepared me for how disarmed and defenceless I felt.

The imagination can be a powerful thing. Just as when we are children it is what we imagine about what we don't know that is frightening, for example: what might be out there in the dark, not the dark itself. So it was with my imagination and my flashbacks. I was not there when Mark abused, but my mind had begun, unconsciously at first, to create an idea of what had happened. The blanket in the back of the wrecked car was the first seed. The never-forgotten photo of Lisa Marie I am sure was there too. Images emerged and were expressed in my thoughts, and sometimes only in my physical being.

It was a lovely spring day and the children loved to go to the park. Grace ran ahead and Joseph was keen to escape from his buggy as we could see the playground ahead of us. Releasing Joseph into the bright sunshine beyond the thicket leading to the park, he ran off in hot pursuit of his sister. As I moved forward, in the cover of the trees, the image shot fully present into my mind's eye: A blanket spread wide beneath the shady canopy of trees, and on the blanket a man and a small child were poised. I blocked the picture forming in my head. But another stronger image formed: I could see Lisa Marie standing underneath the tree, stripped down to her underwear, staring off across the open field. Overcome by the vividness, I was jolted back to reality by the voices of the children, who had now reached the playground and needed my help to lift the latch gate. As I watched them play, thoughts of Mark bringing little girls to places like this intruded. I could not help but wonder once again where the blanket had come from and what it had been used for. Still replaying the trauma, expanding on what I did know of that night Mark died, I questioned again if Mark had pulled into a place like this before he crashed, for one last time.

I did not avoid the park, although it would not have been

surprising if that was what happened next. I hoped this flashback was a one off and the images would go away. I told myself that if I ignored these thoughts and distracted myself it would not happen again. But their intensity increased. The images came without any invitation and my reaction to them became physical rather than emotional. I decided I needed some help. Reluctant though I was to admit it, I wondered if I had developed PTSD.

A brief course of cognitive behavioural therapy (CBT) did help. My therapist taught me the skills to handle and understand what I was experiencing. He could not reverse the clock, but it was possible to redress my responses. I had been pushing the difficult thoughts and feelings away, when what I needed to do was to invite them in. I had to try and sit with them a while; to explore the detail. Only then would they lose their power over me. I will never forget Lisa Marie, but it helped to know my friend Jess, who saw her photo too, feels the same. I was not cured but a pervasive work in progress, but perhaps had not realised or accepted this yet. I could still be taken asunder; my assassin did return.

Summer 2010
Once a year, during the summer term, the whole school goes to the beach for the day. Grace was excited: this would be her third 'beach day' at the school. The previous two had created some happy carefree memories. The sun was shining and it had the makings of a wonderful day. We had forgotten the required bucket and spade, and so stopped to buy one in the little village shop on our way to school. Now we were fully prepared. As we drew up in the turning circle in front of the

school, it was clear something had happened. I caught a glance of a notice on the board outside the school gate and noted that some of the children were in uniform not their beach clothes. Maybe they have had to cancel beach day, I thought; it was hard to think why: the conditions seemed perfect. I got the attention of a passing mum. She explained it had been posted on the school website last night: beach day was cancelled out of respect for a little girl in reception class who had died.

Seeing the other children in their uniforms, Grace began to get nervous in her shorts and t-shirt. I had once made a mistake about the timing of a non-uniform day. She had arrived at school mistakenly dressed as a princess for World Book Day a week early; she remembered this so well. Leaving the bucket and spade in the car, we walked to the gate. Grace became more nervous. Could we go home and collect her uniform? Perhaps, in hindsight, we should have. Instead, I tried to reassure her: other children were in shorts too, she wouldn't be alone.

As we walked toward Grace's class, I overheard someone speak: 'Doesn't the atmosphere of the whole school feel different today, it is so quiet.' Emotions were running high. I saw the red-eyed teachers trying hard to collect themselves and show a brave face. Parents spoke and speculated in hushed tones around me. Grace seemed bewildered. I began to feel flustered and suddenly I was back there. All the physical sensations of that first morning, awash with the fresh news that Mark had died, came flooding over me: the morning three years earlier when I had numbly delivered the children to their nursery classrooms. As I had passed through the glass corridors and classrooms, back then there had been hushed speculation and eyes had looked down, avoiding any contact. My heart began to race, my hands shook. I thought I might be sick. Today: a death, a suicide, unexplained circumstances. Something shocking had come to pass here. A child had been found dead in her bed; her mother had taken her own life.

Tears fell as I helped Grace hang her coat and school bag. I sat heavy hearted on the bench beneath the coats and looked up at Grace, trying my hardest to conceal my reaction. I felt very self-conscious. I worried that other parents would think I was over-reacting or, worse still, making this about me. I was shocked by the physical connection I felt with the atmosphere in the school that morning. My body was in tune with whatever was happening. I was not thinking yet. By the time I reached the classroom door, I could not stop the tears or the shakes.

The teacher pulled me aside, and suggested I talk to someone. She said, 'When I heard this news, you were the first family in my thoughts, I immediately thought of you.'

I was relieved: she understood why I felt and reacted this way.

A psychologist had been brought into the school that morning to support them in managing the response to this event. I told him what had happened this morning as I had arrived at the school and why I thought I had reacted the way I had. He encouraged me to recognise what had happened as a flashback: part of PTSD. I had experienced a visceral response: something physical without initial awareness of the connecting thought or feeling. Hearing him use that diagnosis seemed to give validity to the idea I had experienced a 'trauma'.

Leaving the school, I passed several policemen who had gathered at the gates. I thought briefly of the raid. I realised how numb I had been back then, as I worried about what my neighbours had seen, gathered outside our home with the police. But my body had not forgotten what words and even tears failed to describe.

When I was a little girl, I watched a weekly evening nature programme with my family. One episode stays with me; it was all about scorpions, and the narrator built up a story of these nasty venomous creatures. I sat terrified as a lady innocently slipped her feet into her slippers and was promptly stung by the scorpion concealed within. The nature expert assured us that scorpions are rare in the British Isles, preferring warmer climes. My childhood imagination had already been kindled. I heeded his advice: for those in countries where scorpions do reside, shaking your slippers, checking under bath mats and in baskets of clean and warm laundry are sensible precautions. For years, after that one programme, I somewhat irrationally checked all of the aforementioned hiding places.

And so it is ironic that in ten years living in a warm and humid climate in America, notoriously inhabited by these divisive little creatures, I had never seen a single scorpion; that is until after Mark died. We had laughed about my irrational fear, avoidant behaviour and precautionary measures against this venomous insect. But understanding my phobia, had Mark tracked down and removed scorpions in our home to protect me? Despite the relative prevalence of poisonous creatures in our area I had felt safe. Was it just bad luck that in the three short months before we returned to England I met three scorpions of varying size and terror? My world had become less safe. I had to face my fear of scorpions head on and only I alone could do this. A copy of the Oxford English Dictionary (unabridged) and my own heavy stomping achieved the desired result; I spared my three assailants no compassion.

CHAPTER 16

Holidays and Benchmarks

2009-2011

'The Secret Garden was what Mary called it when she was thinking of it. She liked the name, and she liked still more the feeling that when its beautiful old walls shut her in no one knew where she was. It seemed almost like being shut out of the world in some fairy place ...'
From The Secret Garden by Frances Hodgson Burnett

As a child I loved the story of The Secret Garden, and my children love it too. We were delighted to discover our own version of the imagined garden when we visited the Sand Rose Project, a holiday retreat for bereaved families in Cornwall. This holiday was such a blessing to us, as we tried to work out how to enjoy a family holiday in the midst of so much loss. Just like Mary in the novel, this haven created a space in which we could laugh, cry, love, have fun and remember.

The garden reminded us of the goodness of nature, its

beauty and poise. From the cobbled lane, a bright-red door opened into a cottage paradise. The garden stretched forward from the house, with its winding path and countless nooks and crannies down to the sea. At the bottom of the lush grass slope stood a folly, a castle in miniature, with upstairs views of the majestic waves of the bay, and in the distance the island across the causeway. This hexagonal sunlit room was designed to provide a quiet space. The project did not provide counsellors; the only therapy needed was the place itself – being in touch with nature, connecting with the inner child in the games we played and feeling together as a family. My little ones spent hours gathering up shiny stones and hidden glass pearls into buckets around the fountain, while I relaxed on the lawn nearby. We crossed the causeway to the neighbouring island at low tide and laughed when wellies filled with water as we reached the far shore in the nick of time. I was bathed in the beautiful sound of my children's laughter as they chased their shadows in the stone courtyard of the castle on the mount.

The hexagonal upstairs room of the folly had been set aside as a place for quiet contemplation. I was struck by its strong walls and an overwhelming sense of the presence of those who also understood loss and had visited this place. The folly was a place that had born witness to the grief of all the families who had come to the Sand Rose Project. Next to the harshness of a rough sea, this was a place of refuge, whose silent walls heard the cries and absorbed the tears. I indulged my imagination that if hands could reach out from these old stone walls they would be sturdy, resilient and sure. They would cradle the sorrow and caress the joyful memories shared in this space.

But the power of this bolthole was that it did not hear or offer empty words. Instead, there was an assurance of something that goes beyond what can be seen, and can only be felt. I hoped that Grace would speak to me in the folly; where better to connect. I was desperate to be offered a window into her grief.

17 May 2009, there is still a chill in the evening air. I have brought with me a colouring and activity book that might encourage a conversation. The turning waves crash on the rocks just below. The sea is majestic; the shadows of the island ever present on the horizon. Grace chooses to make a balloon tag on which she can write a note to her dad.

As she colours, the questions hesitantly emerge: 'Mummy, where was Daddy going when he had the accident?' 'Why didn't he tell us where he was going?' 'I think he ran away.'

'Grace, you may be right, he ran because he felt bad about what had happened.'

'Mummy, I think he went because he didn't want to upset you, Mummy, or because he thought you would be upset with him.'

The explanation reeks of the forewarnings that closely guarded their secret. I reply, 'I don't think there was anyone that Daddy was upset with other than himself.'

We colour in silence for a bit as I search for the words I need. 'Grace, do you think about what happened?'

She is looking down, it is a struggle. 'Sometimes in bed I feel good and bad.' A pause. 'Bad because I did those things Daddy wanted me to do; but good because I tried hard not to do them. I told Daddy I didn't want to. There were the other ones;

Daddy had pictures of them doing it, to show me. One of the girls was much older. She ought to have known better how to be good.'

She is just six years old and her words sound so grown up. It is all I can do not to cry. I hold my nerve. 'I am so sorry Grace that those things happened to you. It is not your fault. Daddy was the grown-up. I am not angry with you. I am proud of you for being able to tell me about it. I love you so very much.'

The folly's heavy stone walls conceal our thoughts and fears as silently tears begin to fall and I hold Grace in my arms. When I am alone later my mind reels. It is hard to hear these few snippets of closer detail from Grace; I struggle to take it all in and not to wonder how much more is yet to be revealed.

We had shared holidays with my mum the first year and kept things very simple. She too was feeling the impact of being a widow and had never been on holiday without my dad before. But part of me dreaded becoming that single woman with her mother cliché. A year later, I attempted to do something on my own with the children. It was supposed to be an adventure, instead it was the worst experience of all. Inspired by the success of our time at Sand Rose and wooed by the charming tales of family holidays in a camper, where children play outdoors and life slows to a more manageable pace, I booked a campsite and rented a vintage VW camper van. I was certainly not a seasoned driver of larger vehicles – my own choice of car had always been the smallest and most compact available – so I was shocked when we arrived at the camper rental site, an old and run down farm, with a makeshift office in an outbuilding and a line of genuinely 'vintage' campers.

Desperate not to show my concern to the children, I laughed about the rusty exterior, the high climb into the driver's seat and the heavy and larger-than-can-be-imagined steering wheel and gear stick. I was determined not to be overwhelmed. After a brief and rudimentary lesson in the mechanics and nuances of old van driving, I was handed the keys.

Apprehensive, I drove away down the bumpy country lane stippled with potholes. I was physically challenged by every gear change, as I stretched and jerked the van into motion. The children felt a world away, strapped into the bench seat behind me. We rattled our way, as we embarked on this adventure. My sweaty hands clenched the wheel so tightly, as my knees shook beneath the dashboard. I was hot but I didn't dare take off my cardigan or open a window for fear of losing control or grinding to a halt. And so I sweated on.

The brief drive out to the motorway and subsequent countless lane changes were not long enough for me to gain confidence in driving this monster of a machine. Nothing prepared me for the way the van whipped across lanes as the wind caught it side on. It was all I could do to hold a straight path in the inside lane. I have never driven as slowly as I did that day, nor irritated more other drivers, as we crept toward the New Forest. I was terrified. I felt certain we were all going to die in that van. Grace, sensing my fear, tried hard to reassure me and encourage. I was so relieved to reach the edge of the forest and hear the children exclaim with wonder at the wild horses that roam there. But by now I was so overwhelmed; it took me days to not feel the layers of helplessness building on top of me. I felt very alone.

My confidence shattered, I seemed unable to rise above the simplest of challenges. When we arrived, the awning poles were damaged and the van would not lock. My capacity for calm single-parenting was crushed.

The van was cold and leaky. At night, the roof dripped cold condensation onto our faces, as we shivered under a duvet, just a few inches below the dripping ceiling in the top bunk. Still shocked and needing sleep, I had a horrible argument with a good friend who had planned to join us. She had arrived much later than planned after our disastrous afternoon – only just in time for dinner – and all I could muster at this point was to shut down into emotional 'preservation mode'. I could not express or share my disappointment; I felt cheated of my imagined retreat and by our 'limping' family holiday. I was stuck in my head ruminating on all our loss and pain. My friend left the next morning. I managed three nights in the van before throwing in the towel.

But, on the last night, all packed up and ready to flee, I was brought back to solid ground by a young single mother in a neighbouring tent. Sue was staying at the campsite with her mother and young daughter who was a similar age to Grace. They asked me to join them for a 'cuppa', observing that I seemed very alone. Over the several cups of tea that followed, we talked and shared a little of each of our stories.

Listening taught me a great lesson in God-given possibilities and opportunities. Sue described how in the middle of the night, she had packed a small suitcase and, with her then four-year-old daughter, had jumped out the window of their home. She had fled from a physically abusive husband with an equally abusive extended family. She had run for their lives. Until the law could intervene, she had hidden from his detection. Hearing Sue's own trauma and its impact on her and her mum, I felt grounded again in what it is to suffer and struggle together as human beings and survive against the odds. Sue helped me out of my downward spiral. I believe it was no coincidence her pitch was next to my own.

The camper rental company were shocked by my disgust and early return. They could not reimburse nor compensate for my distress. On reflection, I learnt so much from this holiday, and years on might even be able to laugh at how naive, stubborn and proud I could be.

Holidays are different. They remind the widowed parent of all that they have lost. They remind us of lost dreams and expectations. Breaks from the comfort and structure of daily routine as a single parent can be incredibly isolating. It feels as if holiday parks are full of 'happy families': dads teaching their children to swim, kick a football or ride a bike. Lost dreams are unavoidable when pitched against glimpses of happy 'quads' cycling or picnicking out of wicker baskets on checked tablecloths in the forest. There are children piggybacked home on their father's broad shoulders. Everyone else's world seems perfect even if it is not. A kind of mental filtering goes on where you do not take in the disgruntled teen or disengaged father at the hotel breakfast table.

Grief kept at a distance is brought into the palpable realm. What you no longer have, or never knew, stares you down in each small challenge. Ironically, I know Mark would have been a hopeless camper.

Returning to work there was the inevitable question: 'Did you have a lovely holiday?' I returned no more refreshed or resourced. The van holiday left me bitterly disappointed although I can, of course, laugh about it now.

Holidays were not the only reminders or milestones that had the potential to remind me of all we had lost. Returning to the UK, I had promised myself I would never fall back into the trap of climbing the career ladder. I was not going to re-join the rat race and prioritise career over family. I had now been awarded my MRCGP, the necessary UK qualification for family doctors, yet I had an overwhelming sense that I was meant to work in palliative care. I could not turn my back on this. I wanted to feel I had potential again, to feel I had goals and a future, but I was relatively unqualified to move on in this work in the UK. I wanted to restore this sense of self. I decided to fight for my 'certificate of equivalence', my only realistic path back to being a consultant in my field again.

It was a huge undertaking, punctuated by misunderstanding and difficulty translating skills across the Atlantic; two countries divided by a common language. I was required to document and evidence my skill in unprecedented detail. I needed the help of my former colleagues as well as my current team. I had to ask for their help again; I felt I had already asked for so much support. The process brought back a lot of reminders of all I had achieved, and just what I had let go of when I left the USA. I had developed a career in ethics and in palliative medicine working in a fast-paced university hospital, at the coal face of the lives of those devastated by trauma and illness. I had reached a point in my career where my experiences could be used to teach others. I was given the chance to develop new programmes, connections and resources. I had been able to find a way of marrying my interests in the arts, humanities and medicine. My career had excited me.

In this soul destroying process, I found myself grieving for my career, feeling angry and at times regretting my return to the UK. It took over two years, two trips to the USA and the weight of several trees in paper to process my 400-page application. I think, in some respects, it became a vehicle for me to express some of my anger towards Mark and his actions. I felt the sting of rejection when my first application was declined because of the wrong type of evidence. Financially, I questioned if I was doing the right thing; it was a costly route. Then on Grace's birthday in 2011, I received the phone call while at the supermarket to say my second application had been successful. I wept standing in the checkout.

It is hard to be kind to ourselves in our loss. I had certain expectations of myself and how life 'should be'. I wanted to feel grounded again but life felt so different, and we were irrevocably changed. I had not allowed myself time to grieve the less obvious losses, or given thought to putting in safety nets to foreseeable challenges, like holidays and parents' evenings alone. Certain things intimidate or have the power to make me feel more alone than I am: DIY, financial decisions, computer glitches, Facebook or Instagram, dinner parties, and of course parenthood is by far the greatest tyrant. I am David and these are my Goliaths. It is important for me to recognise that I would not be human if I did not experience further bumps along this road, and that I have not been singled out for challenge; everyone has their own nemesis.

CHAPTER 17

Cards That Fall Like Dominoes

"Who cares for you?" said Alice, (she had grown to her full size by this time.) "You're nothing but a pack of cards!"

At this the whole pack rose up into the air, and came flying down upon her: she gave a little scream, half of fright and half of anger, and tried to beat them off . . .'
From Alice's Adventures in Wonderland by Lewis Carroll

Addicts have no regard for the consequence of their actions. Mark might have felt remorseful that he had drawn Grace into his world, but I do not believe for a minute that he, or anyone, could really fathom how far-reaching the consequences of his self-gratifying actions would reach. They were no more contained in the darkest recesses of our home than a bomb exploding on a busy commuter street.

My mother hates going to the beach. Even if you create an

oasis of rugs and towels, your sandwiches have an unexpected crunch, and as you dry yourself you can't help but find grains of sand between your toes. When you get home from a day at the beach, sand becomes the irritating and unwelcome guest in every little space it can find. Even days later, sometimes longer, you might turn out a shoe or a bag and find grains of hidden sand, or a gritty shell in an old jacket pocket. Pornography and abuse had become the 'unwelcome guests' in our lives, whose consequences knew no bounds. We had our very own tumbling pack of cards.

Every night before I go to bed, like most parents, I check on my children. One night, almost a year after Mark had died, after a difficult evening; I crept into Grace's room to tuck her back in. As I lifted the duvet back over her, she stirred a little and muttered, before loudly saying 'Daddy?' and drifting back to sleep. I feared the worst. That single word of alarm took my thoughts to places I did not want to go. I saw fear in her eyes even if really it wasn't there. Questions, questions: Did Mark visit her at night? Was he such a predator?

As I looked back at photographs of that time I saw only the dark circles under her eyes. How powerful my imagination is; I could not help but wonder if she went to bed afraid. Bedtime was and remains a never-ending challenge; the reluctance to go to bed a constant source of conflict. Is this why? Or was her call to 'Daddy' that night simply because when she is cross with me she wants him more, just as any child might set one parent against another? It is so hard not to push for answers to all of these disturbing questions. I needed patience. A few weeks later, a conversation came out of the blue.

It was bedtime and we had just finished reading, from

Grace's children's Bible, the story of the Creation, and so naturally a conversation about snakes, the devil and Eden ensued! Before I knew it, Grace had embarked on what was only our third conversation about Daddy and what had happened. As I tried not to lead my daughter's thoughts and memories or give her words where there were none, hesitantly, Grace told me how she had not liked the pictures of the children drinking from their daddies or kissing their daddies' bottoms. Carefully, I asked about the pictures. Many were older girls but some were little like her. There was one little girl, like her, whose daddy was bald; our daddy had taken the picture.

Cautiously I ask, 'Did this man come to our home?'

'No,' she pauses, 'only to . . .' she stops herself. Should I have pushed her further? Asked her where? A hotel room perhaps?

Grace reminds me that I had said last summer it was OK to talk, that I did not think she was naughty

'No you are very brave little one. You are not bad. Mummy is sad that these things happened to you.'

The conversation continued cautiously. 'I didn't like drinking from daddy or kissing his bottom.'

'Did this happen very much?'

'Lots and for a long time. Before Joseph was born, when Mummy went to work.'

It would be many more months before we talked again. Like sand in the hour glass, it could not be forced.

A year later, I was to truly realise how pervasive abuse can be in robbing the innocence of others. Grace and my friend's twin sons were sitting on top of the wood pile in the garden, sharing stories from their day. The boys had been to the park that morning and some older boys had heckled them. They wanted to know if they masturbated, hoping no doubt to embarrass them. As the boys explained to Grace what this meant, she innocently replied that she knew all about that; she had done that with her daddy. Returning to their play, no more was said, until that evening at dinner after we had gone home.

My friend and her children were playing a game when the boys told their mum that 'she sucked' at the game they were playing. Reprimanding their use of the word suck, she was floored when, after a brief hesitation, one of the twins said that Grace had told them she had sucked her daddy. Shocked by their casual but innocent reference to Grace's experience, she quickly tried to move the conversation on; trying to protect her even younger daughter, and needing time to think how to address this with two seven-year-old boys.

That evening, I had a phone call to let me know what had happened. It was a shock. Grace was thinking and talking about what had happened. But what was she thinking and who was she talking to? I felt terrible that I had forced my friend and her husband into having to explain these conversations to their children. I was jolted into another reminder of how this sordid matter would reach into other innocent lives. My hold on being normal and leading an ordinary life felt fragile again.

This disclosure had all sorts of ramifications. Until this point, I had waited for Grace to bring conversations up with me and I had not gone to her. I had decided I did not need to persist in finding counselling for her. I had chosen not to tell the school about her abuse. I had not told the parents of her school friends. I did not want Grace to be labelled, avoided or treated differently. I worried what others might think of us as a family. I worried about preserving both my children's innocent picture of the daddy they had lost. I feared gossip and small mindedness. But now bigger than all of this was a new responsibility – to other people's children; to preserve their innocence and not let the paedophiles' pervasiveness stretch any further in its destructive wake.

First, I sought out advice: the Lifecentre came back into our lives. I was given practical advice about how to talk to Grace about what had happened with the boys. They felt she was still too young to have formal counselling at just six years old. I needed to balance resetting Grace's boundaries for telling her story of what had happened while not making her feel different or wrong, or that she should not talk at all. I needed to explain that it is alright to talk about these things but that it needs to be to the right people. I did not want to leave Grace believing that there are some secrets we just cannot tell. She had heard this message before, just like many abused children before her. I had to find the words; no one was giving me a script.

Thankfully, I realised, I did not have to tell everyone all at once. Indeed, I didn't have any obligation to tell anyone at all. It is my choice. The Lifecentre counsellor suggested teachers did not automatically need to know, only if it would inform a situation or problem.

When you have such barbed news, it is hard, especially in the moment of crisis, not to treat this like a hot potato: to be passed quickly from one person to another. A good lesson to learn is to hold on to the information for a while, to consider the need to pass it on, and to let it percolate. Then, as the intensity of the need wains, somehow it becomes clearer if it is imperative to share.

I told the headmistress. She was very supportive. She too was measured in her response, putting Grace: the child, ahead of Grace: the victim; not wanting to create a label, and for this reason weighing up the need to tell others in the school. This remains a dilemma every year: do Grace's teachers need to know? I find that mostly this has been handled very sensitively, and I have never felt my trust has been abused. But even so, with each new relationship I travel with trepidation.

Amid my own grief and the challenges of helping Grace settle into the newness of everything in her life, perhaps I missed a vital clue that secrets might be our stumbling block. As I prepared to finish this book and I was gathering together my many scribbled notes, I stumbled on a memo from Grace's teacher that I had not noticed before. It was April 2008, Grace was five years old. The note reads: 'Had quite a tearful day. Wanted to tell another child a secret; I think it is a way to get a friend on her own. Hope this is OK.'

As I read this message my heart sinks. Why was Grace tearful? Did I miss a massive red flag? This feels far from 'OK'. A five-year-old with a secret plan or idea is not so unusual; indeed Grace's friend cooked up a secret plot to meet the fairies at midnight in the park and got as far as the front door with a bag of snacks for her travels. But a five-year-old who has been abused, who has been told to keep a special secret; a little girl who desperately wants to belong, to be loved and liked. Who does not understand the impact of her secret. She would want to tell.

Talking to Grace about the 'wood pile chat' seemed to go well. I thought I had balanced the need to keep her door to talking to me and those adults she might trust far enough ajar, for her to feel she did not need to hold secrets, while creating tighter boundaries around talking to other children. The need to tell other parents diminished. For about a year, the lid remained firmly closed on our can of worms.

In the summer of 2010, all traumatised by the premature end to our camper van holiday, I called my brother from a roadside pit stop and spontaneously joined him and his family on their holiday at a beach house not far from where we lived. My children adore spending time with their cousins; Grace in particular feels in tune with her cousin, Mae. This brief diversion gave me the opportunity to talk over my van experience and feel a little restored. The August weather was not especially kind to us: the sea was rough, the wind blew in gusts and brought with it the cold and rain. But I watched with reassurance as Grace and my brother body-surfed despite the conditions in the sea. We were struck by the determination and resilience of my young daughter that afternoon, as she did battle with the brutal waves, keen to master the board. Maybe she would be alright.

A few days later, I received a hesitant phone call from my sister-in law. My niece had seemed inexplicably upset for several days since the beach retreat. Gently her parents had coaxed out of her the reason for her distress. Grace had told her about her dad and what they had done. Mae did not know what or how to make sense of this – she felt hurt and a profound sadness for Grace. We do not know what prompted this disclosure. They had been showering after being in the sea. They are close and share with each other their troubles and support each other in ways we as grown-ups cannot. Shaken, I realised I had not been effective in resetting Grace's boundaries. I needed professional help.

Grace attended four sessions at the Lifecentre with the child therapist. She was now eight years old, but she disclosed very little. She played with the sand trays and drew pictures of butterflies, for a second time. She came to the point of resenting the disturbance these sessions created in her normal school day. She struggled to understand why she was there. Looking back, we did reach a point of closing the net of safe disclosure. I think she now knows who she can talk to when she wants to talk about the abuse; but I cannot be certain of this or anything. She simply does not talk. She is increasingly private. Since the sessions, she has never begun a conversation about 'daddy'. How do you tell your child on one hand that it is OK to talk, and on the other it is important you pick wisely who you talk to? Had I in fact closed the book for some time to come?

As Grace and I now enter the arena of her teens, new battles create a further minefield for our emotions. I am filled with fear for the trappings of the internet and modern technology. I cannot help myself in my desperate attempts to protect my children. Parental controls and boundaries around such devices have created much tension in our home. When we argue, I struggle not to see Mark in Grace's face. Or, worse still, sometimes the face of the child who was abused, who once again feels her boundaries violated.

Sometimes, she has a disassociated look of fear about her, even in the absence of any threat. When our relationship is challenged by distrust or fights for control, I am plagued by uncertainty. Does my daughter behave the way she does because she is struggling for normal teenage independence, or is there an undercurrent that comes from the stain of her abuse? When she lies to me, I wonder if she learnt to lie in that web of abuse, and if I can undo the harm that has been done. I cannot help but allow the pessimistic predictions about the future of an abused child to feed my thoughts, or the suppositions of others based on what they see. When she communicates what she feels, she struggles to express her feelings in anything but a rage of injustice. Does this come from the anger she feels deep inside for what happened to her and for experiences beyond words?

I am filled with sadness for a situation beyond my control. Increasingly, I find myself angry with the man I cannot hold to account. I find hope in her determination and resilience so far. And in knowing that she is much loved.

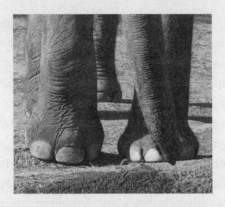

STEP SIX Indigestion

Six thousand and three hundred kilograms is a lot of meat, especially for a relapsed vegetarian.

In the beginning, the tough hide took days to chew over. Eventually, larger portions presented themselves and sat like boulders in my throat, strangling the life out of me. And when solid matter met acid in my gut, my chest felt heavy and a searing pain between my breast plates cut me in two, disturbing the peace of the night.

The doctor diagnosed indigestion. Some reflux was inevitable. Could I change my diet? Reduce the acid? Digest more slowly?

The advice: smaller pieces of elephant taken with the tiniest of spoons. It was important not to always eat alone; as you might imagine there were plenty of portions to share. But in reality, I had to consume the majority. At times my appetite was lost; I seemed trapped in my own form of gluttony. Companionship slowed the pace and a temporary change of diet brought perseverance.

Keep upright. In the midst of uncertain terrain it is easy to lose your footing and fall backward into a veritable abyss. Friends provided ladders to see me out of the pit and scaffold to see me across the wide chasms which formed.

At the close of the meal, my hands and feet were stained. These were indelible marks. Even with the grace of time, my gut still reacted to fresh nourishment; elephant had been my habitual diet for so long.

In the desert, I longed to wash off the dust and grime; to run towards the horizon where an oasis might be revealed. Out of the shadows, I hoped to hear my children laughing and playing and to join them in mirage fountains of fresh water. There, at a distance from the corpse, they would not sink into the deep elephant footprints which remained, nor find their own elephants. It was not their time to consume such things.

CHAPTER 18

Meeting a Paedophile

Spring 2010

It is the nature of working as a GP that you never really know what is about to walk through your door. Nothing prepared me for this ten-minute consultation. It had been a busy afternoon surgery and I had still several more patients to see. Thinking back, there was something about this forty-year-old man, in his stiff office attire, that reminded me of Mark from the moment he entered the room. He began by saying he had come to ask for a referral for a 'problem' but it was not immediately evident what the 'problem' was. It must have taken a lot of guts to come and ask.

This was a married man, the father of two young boys and a new baby girl and he worked in IT. He took a few minutes to explain what he was asking for – help for a serious addiction to sexual websites: pornography and sexual chat rooms. He relaxed a little and the story unfolded, as I tried desperately to remain engaged with his story. Just beneath the surface, I was really trying to work out how I felt about this.

He had recently lost his job after he had been discovered looking at 'Adult' sites at work. He went on to explain his addiction, spending hours each day consumed by this material. Forced to relocate his family, he had shared the reason for his dismissal with his wife, who was supportive, and subsequently with his parents. I found myself wanting to ask, Why? Do you look at extreme sites? What about children? But I remained professional throughout.

I survived the consultation and made the referral. I had to move on to the next patient and remain in control. I was shaken but I felt encouraged that I had not fallen apart.

It struck me afterwards that this felt like an opportunity. I had not had the opportunity to understand or talk to Mark about his addiction. Now, it was disturbing to have what felt like a fantasy conversation with Mark; the similarities were unnerving. But was God giving me the opportunity to forgive? There was no closure with Mark, and to forgive someone you can no longer have it out with seemed impossible. But this was real. And furthermore, perhaps, I could be a small part of a man's recovery from this addiction. I packaged this up in the positive, but told myself this man was nothing like Mark and moved on to the next challenge.

But it was not going to end there. Six weeks later, I received a phone call from this patient's counsellor. He thought my patient might need medication to help with his addiction. The details began to hang heavy on the bare bones of the story. My patient had not lost one but two jobs previously because of his addiction. In the last month, he had been unable to resist the pull back to viewing interactive sites with fourteen-to-sixteen-year-olds: children. The counsellor was not yet sure the patient could be counselled, but hoped he would continue to come to his sessions. Could I see my patient to discuss medication?

Children: the counsellor did not seem perturbed by the idea that this man was interacting with children. As a GP, I had responsibilities to protect children from harm. I could not ignore what I had just been told. This man had lied to both of us initially about the content he was viewing; were there more details he had yet to disclose? I felt conflicted with the counsellor. Was my own experience tainting my approach to this case? I acknowledged to him that this case was difficult for me, but I did not say why. I began to feel nervous. He acknowledged my challenge, but he felt that he, as the therapist, needed to remain in the patient's confidence. He wished he had not told me the details. The call came to a close with regret: if someone was going to report this, the patient would need to know. The therapeutic relationship was at risk. The words on the papers on my desk began to swim on the page. I was going to fall apart.

I sat stunned. The clock ticked loudly in the background. In that moment, I was unable to continue with the other mounds of paperwork that lay scattered on my desk in front of me. It was getting late. Tears rolled down my face and my body shook. I could not hold back. Should I have told the counsellor why this is difficult for me? Is my judgement cloudy? Surely, I cannot be objective in this case. It is too personal. How can I believe and trust again and risk getting it wrong? Shouldn't I trust my gut feeling? I had been naive before. I became more disturbed as I thought through what had been said in this telephone call: what if he was looking at my child? Anyone's child?

An hour passed of making more mundane phone calls and checking test results. When our practice nurse walked into the room, I was still not composed for company. My mask was down and I burst into tears, and my situation flooded out. I had to widen the net in that moment, and allow others to know why I felt so compromised by this situation.

The net had to be thrown out further. I needed a colleague to take over the situation I found myself consumed by. I could not be confident that I would be impartial in this man's case. It felt too close to home; how could I not fall prey to bias? And the potential for harm to myself seemed too great as what was emerging was an almost certain trigger for flashbacks and more anxiety. It didn't feel fair to either of us that I continue to manage his case. The response from my GP colleague was matter of fact. As he was on-call and staying late, he would call the police child protection team for advice. Once we had established with this team what needed to happen next, I would call the patient and explain that I might need to report the situation for child protection reasons. My colleague had skilfully delegated this responsibility back to me to talk to the patient; I had made an error in not forewarning my patient I could not keep his confidence if I felt he were a risk to others. It was acknowledged that even if he did not give me permission to breach his confidentiality, I was obligated to do so. Before formal proceedings could be taken, I needed to explain my obligation to tell with or without his permission; I had a duty of care to him.

The idea of talking to this man again terrified me. Could I

do this without appearing anxious? Could I remain professional and unemotional? Part of me wanted to see it through, despite the fear, and my colleague did not offer to step in. I felt conflicted. I told myself, I am a professional I should be able to handle this. And yet, I am not objective, someone else should take over. A conflicting internal dialogue ensued. Am I denying this man a chance? Not all men who look at pornography are like Mark. But I struggled to believe this – I had deceived myself before.

I had difficulty sleeping that night, disturbed by thoughts of the past, and Grace woke twice with bad dreams. My work had not challenged me in this way for some time. Shortly after I started work again in the UK, a woman came in to see me whose son had just been killed in a motorbike accident. She was worried about her daughter-in-law, who was the same age as me and a doctor. They too had two small children. Listening to this story of loss and providing some advice for this patient and her family, carried me into my own world of grief. I finished my morning surgery and cried all the way home. This time the feelings were different; this was the trauma that came flooding back. I was challenged to revisit my feelings about Mark and about my own judgement.

Mark's infrequent intrusion into my senses since he died has been unexpected. But on this night, in the midst of restless sleep, there he was in full-face, unmistakeable at the glass window. My dream had projected me forward to my final day at the practice. Standing in the reception area to call in my next patient, I heard the voice first and then his face drew my attention. 'Hello honey, I thought I would come and wish you well.'

Within seconds, I was stunned into wakefulness and dread. It felt so real. Was he alive? As consciousness took control, I recognised the experience as a dream, supporting thoughts and images built the reality: a mangled car, keys stained with blood, the death certificate: he must be dead. I calculated lying there in the dark: two years, nine months, thirty days and five hours since that moment. I remembered when I diligently counted the days and then slowly the months. Now time passing was marked by these arresting jolts or fantasy flashbacks.

The police showed little interest in the initial phone call from my colleague. They felt they would already know of the family if there were significant concerns. Their own surveillance of internet sites would have flagged this man up if his activities were illegal. They commented that a lot of these 'young girls' on pornography sites are older than they seem.
We were advised to just keep things medical for now. If we had concerns about his 'actual' children then we should inform child protection services. I started my patient on an antidepressant.

I felt angry, let down and disgusted by their lack of interest. I wanted more to be done but I was not sure what. I reprimanded myself for failing to remain objective, but a little niggle told me that perhaps my experience gave me extra insight into the situation.

I found myself wondering why God had put me in this situation. Was this an opportunity for me to heal? Was I being asked to understand or forgive? Or was it that I was here so that I could see just how far I had come, how much stronger I was than three years earlier?

A week later, I was contacted by a member of the child protection team. They had decided to investigate the case. I would have to let the patient know and breach his confidentiality by giving his name for the investigation. I worried that we had all got it wrong and I had started a series of events that were going to change a family's life. I knew what that meant. I shuddered as they explained that I needed to speak to my patient's wife in the first instance, not the patient, to ensure she can pick up the tale-tell signs of a problem. I thought, If only someone could have forewarned me. But what would this have meant for us?

I phoned 'the wife' and it was as if the tables were being turned. She was angry, defensive and obviously upset by my call. I wanted to reach out and say that 'I understand'. She was guarded and protective of her husband. I got this. She spoke of how her husband's counselling the day before had been challenging and difficult. She was trying to be patient because she hoped to be able to go along too in a few weeks. She explained that they had not been able to afford counselling before; especially when her husband had lost his job.

As she spoke, I felt guilty for reporting them. She was full of hope. Reporting them could be damaging to the progress they had made, to their trust of each other and any faith in the system in place to help them with this addiction.

I went off sick with nausea and overwhelming fatigue, but I still had to call my patient. Time was running short – it was something I couldn't avoid. He too was angry: he felt his confidentiality had been breached. He had trusted. He had stepped out and made himself vulnerable, looking for support and help. He had been assured by his therapist that, as long as he did not act on his impulses, his disclosures would go no further. I tried to explain that some disclosures between professionals are necessary. As I listened, I sensed that he felt like the victim in this. He felt wronged. In that moment, I felt guilty. Mostly, I regretted that I may have shattered the relationship the therapist had established with this man, and any hope for change.

Unaware I had already spoken with his wife, he asked me to speak to her and explain on his behalf. She was angry too. It was as if she had never spoken to me before. 'Just as we make the decision to ask for help, this is what happens . . .' She spoke of how 'she trusted her husband'. She was still trying to believe in him. The consequences of admitting there was a problem were far too great. I tried to reassure them that the investigation was precautionary. As she spoke, I felt churned up again: Am I making them the victims of my own regret? I was so trying not to.

And yet at several points in my conversations with them both, I wanted to scream down the phone the husband's culpability. You did this. Have you forgotten it was you that broke the law? It is you that has this disgusting addiction . . . Not me and not your therapist! If he is innocent in this they have nothing to fear. My head told me that my duty was to protect children: children at home and those virtual children on the internet. I put the phone down and lay my head back on my pillow, contemplating the further fallout from the therapist, who might also feel betrayed. What a mess! But I needed to remember this was not my mess.

I handed in my resignation at the end of this episode. It was not the whole reason for leaving general practice and returning to my career as a hospice doctor, but it certainly played its part in convincing me that it was the right decision at the right time. In my professional life I have to be able to encounter many difficult and challenging aspects of my patients' lives, but it was important to feel more control about how I managed this. We are all only human. I had learnt a valuable lesson in being gentle with myself, not just with others. I realised that I wanted to feel supported by a team where occasional vulnerability is allowed. I am privileged in my current work to find this to be true.

The patient's wife left him a few months later; he lost his new job and he was subject to further investigation by the child protection team. It would emerge that, this time, my instincts were correct.

CHAPTER 19

Travelling Back

September 2011

My next trip back to America was for the evidence file so I could be recognised as a specialist in palliative medicine in England. I hated to leave the children behind this time (they provided a great buffer to the emotions that surfaced returning to where we had lived), but it was a business trip and I needed to focus. And I had another agenda while I was alone: I was going to try and piece together some of what was missing from my memories of Mark and his final days. I was grappling with a better understanding.

Despite this plan, I had still not anticipated my visit, four years on, to be so challenging. I thought I was in a good place emotionally: strong and resilient. But such is the nature of grief. My assailant, sitting on my right shoulder, never gave up and was always ready for attack when my defences were down. It took just a couple of days seeped in old memories for every nerve ending to be laid bare. And by the end of this week, it was as if on every street corner, or at every turn, there was a memory of Mark to be found. I was exhausted, and shocked by the intensity of my feelings so far along the journey back to healing.

I stayed at a retreat owned by some friends, and it became a place of refuge for me. They had created it out of a beautiful old farmhouse and had stunning panoramic views of the surrounding countryside. For me, it is a place where I can feel in tune with nature and where life slows to an easy pace. I spent three very relaxing days there with Anna and her family. The guest house sits high on a hill and from the porch you can watch powerful wide-winged eagles soar through the sky and swoop down into the long field grass to catch their prey. It is a magnificent sight. In uninterrupted peace, I was finding space to write our story; sitting there, I felt firmly in control. I made the rules of engagement.

With nervous energy simmering beneath the surface, I left the retreat feeling strong enough to drive to the place where Mark had died. It seemed ridiculous; the need to visit a remote strip of grass by the side of a road, sixty miles from anywhere. They call this closure, but I'm not sure it really closes anything. Perhaps, it just leaves the door slightly less ajar. I was certainly curious to see for myself, and to create my own version of what I think might have happened on that horrible night. It felt like it was something I needed to 'tick off the list', and that perhaps when it was done, I would feel better.

But I don't. Ridiculously, I find myself wanting to go back for a second look. To confirm or negate what little I saw. It is as if a piece of me needs to stay there; to be there. But of course, I don't think I will ever find what I am looking for on that strip of road: the answers, a last word with Mark, and to know why. I have never returned for that second visit.

The drive on that one trip was really quite lovely. It was a beautiful sun-kissed day and I was following country roads surrounded by forest and fields. There was the occasional country town – not much more than shacks – or an occasional rundown country home with a wrap-around porch, or an isolated country store with stacks of watermelons or ripe peaches around the entrance; all of this felt reminiscent of times gone by. Mark really had died a long way from anywhere.

Despite the rural location and a sense I was driving to the middle of nowhere, this US route was a road that Mark had known well. We had lived in one of the few towns along its path as newlyweds when I first moved to America. Every morning, about 5 a.m., he had taken this route eighty miles south to the air force base, while I had journeyed forty miles in the opposite direction to the hospital, where I was a resident physician. With the help of the accident report and the photographs taken shortly after the crash, I easily found the spot and pulled over.

A state of perplexity came over me. I sat rooted in the car feeling shaky and anxious. I can really say I didn't know what to do or feel. I had anticipated this trip for four years. I wanted to cry but the tears wouldn't come. I had planned to leave a note and a wild rose from the cottage garden at the retreat 'Mark, know that you were loved and that we miss you. Thank you for our two beautiful children. Alice x'. Perhaps I should have said 'you are forgiven'. Would that have helped? I was speechless. I felt numb; an emotion that had become a familiar state of being.

The road was not as straight as I had imagined, as you approach this section from the south, there is a slight turn in the road and the camber is uneven. On the far side, there is a deep ditch, surrounded by arid untamed grasses and bushes. This had provided a stopping point for the Winnebago that had rolled over and onto its roof. A strip of short grass flanked the near side, where Mark's car had come to rest. Mark's vehicle had hit the much larger holiday van head on. It had recoiled and the metal shell had then curled up into a foetal position on the green bank, just short of a tall wire perimeter fence. Here the grass had been burnt by the heat of the spinning wheels.

There were of course no lasting traces of the accident now. The scorched grass had grown new verdant shoots, and although there were some shattered pieces of tyre they belonged to more recent trucks, which naturally shed their rubber as they clip the side of the road. A solitary tree stood just a short distance from this area, its branches providing some scant shade from the unforgiving sun. At its feet, I placed my note and flower, and then deliberated with uncertainty what to do next. I had wanted more from this journey; it had been heavy with expectation.

Nervously, I approached the house which stood back behind the tall wire fence. I hoped someone would be home, someone who could tell me what they had seen that day. Perhaps, I could meet the first man on the scene; the one who had alerted the emergency services and seen or heard Mark's final moments. But it was not to be. After quite a delay, a woman cautiously opened the front door; she had not lived there very long and knew nothing. She quickly closed the door. There was nothing more to say.

Disappointed, I climbed back into the car, where I lingered just a few moments longer at the roadside before reluctantly pulling away; a few tears fell and it began to rain. A man methodically tracked up and down his lawn on a riding mower on the opposite side of the road; a neighbouring house. I felt tempted to stop and ask him if he recalled the accident. I desperately wanted to connect in time with someone. Was this the man who had raised the alarm? Instead I lost my nerve. Slowly, I drove away and my mind indulged itself once more with the thought that, as the road turned, Mark's death had been an accident, not a suicide. There was no certainty or peace in this idea as the observations of Faye and Clare, and the photographs of the car that could not be denied, tainted it. I have resolved that we will never really know. My reconnaisance trip fell short of my anxious expectations. Another much anticipated 'to do' was to speak to Inspector Hutton once more. The inspector was my only other source of detail to hang on my skeleton of knowledge about that summer and the husband I now felt I scarcely recognised or understood. Four years on, I felt the need for reassurance that I had not been protected at the time from some additional horrible truths about Grace's experience, and to hear if there had been any developments in the case. I had not heard from Inspector Hutton since we had left, and hearing his voice jolted me back to all of the emotion of those few encounters years earlier.

I had expected his voicemail and felt flustered as I tried to explain my need to perhaps 'have ten minutes of his time'. But he seemed unhurried and very gracious on this call. He was happy to talk now, although he was unsure he would have a lot to add to the details of the case. He remembered us well. He did not recall holding back any detail from me but felt he had been open and honest about the photos and their content. I enquired if there had been any more developments: 'Your husband's files and internet identity led to a good number of prosecutions and the shutting down of at least three internet forums. At this time, there was nothing to suggest Mark had distributed Grace's pictures or posted them on a forum.' The National Child Victim Identification Program (NCVIP) had the photos on file; as soon as any of these images are found on anyone's computer they would notify the 'victim' via Inspector Hutton, the investigating officer. There had been none such incidents. I should feel relief.

The inspector asked how the children were and I was touched when he asked if I would object to sending him a recent photo of Grace. He would like to see what a beautiful young lady she had become. He described a connection he felt with the few cases in which there was a personal contact with the victim and their family. My call, he told me, was the high point of his week.

Just five days had passed; I was shattered. The plane jolted away from the runway as I savoured the final chapters of the novel I was reading, One Day by David Nicholls. A book provided a welcome retreat; the story engrossed me. I desperately needed a happy ending, but instead tears rolled down my cheeks as I felt shot down in my tracks: she dies. How could this be? The romance was over and Dexter was alone. As I looked out of the window, I could see a river winding its way through fields, escaping the city limits,

stretching far beyond this state and into the next. I was struck
by how this force of nature flowed on, while time seemed to
have stood still in my heart. All that my return trip had
brought to the surface flooded out of me in that moment. I
was leaving and it felt like, if sense and preservation prevailed,
I might never return.

CHAPTER 20

New Daddy Needed

It is, perhaps, widely accepted that you do not miss what you never had. And, certainly at face value, grieving the father you never knew might seem simpler than the fate my daughter was dealt. But, sadly, I do not underestimate the loss and wounds that Joseph also feels and will continue to feel as he thinks of his father.

Unlike Grace, Joseph speaks of his daddy a lot. It began when he was three, when other children at nursery talked about their daddies. He still asks countless questions. I never lie, although sometimes I am challenged in my search for an answer. Sometimes the daddy he imagines is beyond his reality. I fear most for the day when he knows the truth. He has a naive and hopeful expectation and recollection. For Joseph, the daddy who is gone is imagined. He is the daddy of his dreams that he has never known. Sometimes this makes him sad. He is sometimes hungry to identify with something of this man: 'Did Daddy like purple?' 'What was Daddy's favourite food?' 'Do you think Daddy would like my picture?' 'Did Daddy have a license when he crashed his car?' 'Mummy, when I'm older will you be dead?' 'Will you have a big accident like Daddy?'

From a very young age, Joseph spoke openly with his friends about his daddy being dead. They were all very matter of fact. A friend even asked if Daddy was flushed down the toilet like his goldfish. But, at one nursery lunch, Joseph announced to his friends that his daddy was going to come back to life. In compassionate response, his teacher loaned us some story books about loss. Joseph cried as one of the stories came to an end. 'That book makes me sad; I don't like it.' 'Why would my teacher loan us such a sad book, Mummy?' But questions about how Daddy died followed.

Months earlier, we had buried a blackbird in the back garden; I am asked if that is how we buried Daddy? I am catching up, thinking what to say: Well no, Daddy would have been a lot bigger than a bird. We wouldn't have fitted him in the garden like the blackbird.

After a little time to reflect, Joseph draws his own conclusions: 'Oh no, of course not!' It is Easter and my three-year-old little boy narrates his own suppositions, some of which are funny. 'I know what happened Mummy; we found a deep cave and put Daddy in it, then rolled a big stone in front of it.'

Not knowing whether to laugh or cry, I reply, 'Well . . . no, that was a special way of burying Jesus. We didn't bury Daddy or other people that way.' I then draw breath and begin what feels like digging a hole I might have to climb into. 'When

people die their bodies aren't useful to them anymore and...'
Thankfully on this occasion, I was saved from a conversation
about cremation by another flitting thought and a change of
direction.

It is 6 a.m. when I hear the familiar shuffling of little feet
making their way along the hallway into my bedroom. I pull
back the duvet and Joseph climbs in right beside me and
nestles in the crook of my arm. As he wriggles awake, his
thoughts begin to flow: 'Mummy, where are Daddy and
Granddad? When they died, where did they go?'

I pause. Indignation follows. 'You must know Mummy, you
are a doctor!'

It seems I can no longer avoid the cremation conversation.
'Well their bodies were cremated.'

'What's that?'

A pause. 'Well, the bodies are burnt to ashes and that is
cremation.' Short pause. 'But who they were can't be burnt.'

'Is that what the angels come down for?'

Wow, that is a helpful diversion. A conversation follows
about angels and what they might look like. And then we
return to a thought. 'When I die, Mummy, can I have my ashes
sprinkled around the tree like Granddad, and then it will be
Granddad's and Joseph's tree!'

Angels are a topic of some fascination for Joseph. He has
opinions on the subject. I find his ideas challenging to counter
or explain. For Joseph, Daddy and Granddad are angels; they
live in the sky with Jesus and God. When you become an angel,
you also become perfect. This makes Daddy perfect.

I lack his childhood innocence and eagerness to accept

people as he finds them. This is where I get stuck. I want to shift to that place of believing that Mark was forgiven, but can I forgive Mark? While I do think he died overwhelmed with remorse for his actions, I struggle with the idea that he is now at peace when I am not. Indeed, in God's eyes I am not perfect, only a broken human being.

I am most struck by Joseph's loss through the legacy of a picnic in the park with family and friends. Joseph, then aged four, had a fabulous time playing cricket with the other children and one of their dads. He squealed with joy as Sam threw him into the air and caught him in his sturdy hands. I am reminded of how Grace loved her daddy to lift her up.

A few months later, as summer approaches, Joseph wore his favourite checked shirt to nursery. One of the teachers told him he looked handsome and a story unfolded, which he then repeated in more vivid detail to the French conversation teacher who visited weekly.

Joseph told them that his 'new daddy' had bought him the shirt to wear at his mummy's wedding last weekend, because he was the best man. He elaborates: 'Mummy met John her new husband while I was at nursery. I am going to have a "new daddy"!'

When the teacher, Mrs Davis, pulled me aside to enquire about this story I began to cry. It was so unexpected, but perhaps was the symptom of a little boy who missed not having a father so much. A few weeks later, recovered from the initial shock and amusingly impressed by my gifted young storyteller, I had a lot of explaining to do when the French teacher greeted me with exuberant and earnest congratulations!

But on a more serious note, that night after the teacher told me of Joseph's storytelling, I tried to ask casually about the tale, 'Mrs Davis mentioned you were talking about Daddy today?'

My little boy replied, 'Yes I was telling my friend about the games Daddy plays with me.'

Present tense. 'Plays with you?'

He continued, 'Yes, I love him to swing me in the air above his head.'

I then respond to Joseph's emotions not the content: I ask if he misses his daddy. Of course he misses the daddy he never knew. He remembers Sam, his friend's dad. He replied that he would like a new daddy.

'I know it must be hard. I am sorry we don't have a new daddy.'

'Mummy hasn't met anyone yet.' Maybe it will happen when I am bigger.'

He hopes I will. For Joseph it is simple: a daddy is someone to throw you in the air and safely catch you in his arms: a simple enough wish. It is what daddies do. My own sadness reaches further into my grief, as I remember how Mark would lift Grace above his head; she would laugh and he would dare her for a moment 'to touch the sky'.

I, too, indulge in wishful thinking; not just for Joseph but for me as well. I would love to take a chance on loving someone again, but the stakes feel high. After several months of CBT percolating through my mind, one phrase from my wise therapist sits in a stronghold in my head: it is just a coffee! I had built up the idea of dating again into such a high tower to climb. I was standing at the altar before the first date could be allowed conception. Fear of where one brief meeting for a coffee might lead had paralysed any chance of future romantic possibilities. I was afraid.

In the movie Notting Hill the heroine, Anna, meets her romantic hero, William, in a small independent book shop. In the film, Serendipity, a book defies the odds, bringing the boy and girl together for true love to triumph over adversity. It would seem that bookshops and their cafes make the perfect romantic backdrop.

And so an independent bookstore with its own quirky café, should have been the perfect place to begin a new romance. Maybe that was Charlie's thinking when he went to work there in the summer of 2007. But poor Charlie's timing was all wrong.

I had just returned to work after Mark's death. Venturing out in public spaces was still daunting. But a friend invited me to lunch and it provided the ideal opportunity to buy a gift for our much-loved trainee who was leaving: a book on loss. I remember feeling very at ease as I ordered my book from the friendly sales guy behind the counter. I love bookshops and books help me to escape; it felt good to meet 'the me' who could laugh and relax. I had not ventured out in a while. I did not give a second's thought to the service as I handed over my details.

A few days later, I was in the bedroom packing some boxes of Mark's clothes, contemplating what to do with eighteen years of accumulated air force uniforms, when the phone rang. It was Charlie, from the bookstore. He seemed a little nervous but came straight out with it. 'I just wondered if you would come out on a date with me. I thought you seemed so lovely when you came into the store the other day. I know I shouldn't have but I just had to call.'

I was staggered. His timing seemed ludicrous and I was not sure what to say. 'I am flattered Charlie, but I am afraid I will have to say no. My husband died six weeks ago, and I am moving back to England next month.'

A short pause: 'Oh . . . I am sorry. Perhaps if you don't go—'

I interject: 'No I think I will be going. I am sorry: just bad timing. Goodbye.'

I had to laugh. It seemed so funny. I wonder what Charlie thought when he came off that call. I hope his timing improves. That was my one and only invitation in nine years; meeting a man in the bookstore would still be my ideal.

Since then, I have hesitated, despite the passage of time, to re-enter the world of dating. Over and over, I have told myself, It's only a coffee, and yet it feels so much bigger than that. What is scary has grown and morphed so much that I now fear starting again in the world of 'romance' on so many levels. I have not dated in more than fifteen years. It feels odd to imagine going through those awkward firsts again. A first kiss that was or is not Mark is unimaginable. It all feels so much more challenging this time around.

And what makes this worse is that it seems the only way 'in' is via the internet. This in itself is a huge hurdle to tackle. The internet has been the source of a lot of devastation in our lives. I have so many questions and doubts: What if men lie about themselves? What if they are all frauds or worse still all paedophiles? How would I know? I got it so wrong before. Furthermore, how do I sell myself in this two-dimensional platform? I wasn't that great at dating the first time around. Will anyone find me attractive? How can I ever trust? How can I ever expect someone to accept me and my story? How long can I conceal who I am? When to tell? How to tell? I consider and reconsider so much. And all that is before I even get online.

Instead, I am reverting back to the faith method: if it is going to happen it will, regardless of what I do. Just as much as Joseph wants a 'new daddy', I do not want to be alone. My young son states honestly and matter of factly what are my lost dreams too. They make me cry. I want to find him the daddy of his dreams. I worry that, just like me, he wants this too much and we will only be disappointed. But I cannot lose hope. If I do then I will be the victim, and all my demons the victor.

If I had been granted a crystal ball and seen what my future had in store, or if I could rewrite my love story with a happy ending, I might have chosen never to marry Mark. But, and it is a big but: I have two beautiful children who would not be here if I had not stepped out in that fateful direction. I would not be the woman, mother or the doctor I am now without the family and friendships born out from this story.

CHAPTER 21

The Elephant's Shadow

'He called you out of darkness into his wonderful light'
1 Peter 2:9

Spring 2016

In the beginning a part of me did not want time to move on; with each passing day or week that completed, I felt less connected with Mark; that version of Mark who I had loved. It was as if the further we travelled from the day Mark had died, the less likely it was we could turn back and restore a sense of normality. I stopped counting a little while ago, and now I know I want to look forward because I cannot go back. What is done is done. All that remains is what we do next.

I am sometimes struck by how far we and the world in general have come in just nine years. I am stunned now by the passing of time. Since Mark died: civil war has erupted all over the world; children no longer play with toys but instead with mobile gaming screens; and we all listen to music, play films, watch TV and can connect with each other on the go and in an instant. So much has changed and the media, computers and the internet are at the heart of it all.

When I look back on this period of my life, I realise that it is the written and spoken word, and in particular metaphor, that has helped me most. It is in the abstract that it has been easiest to make some awful sense of all that has happened. 'How do you eat an elephant?' It is poignant that the elephant and I can have so much in common. She lives in community, treasures her young and perhaps demonstrates one of the clearest pictures of mourning in the animal kingdom. The elephant cries, stomps and holds firm ground, gets angry, expresses fear and terror and clearly loves. She is a magnificent example to us of the precious gift of motherhood. It is also her magnitude that lends itself so beautifully to a train of thought: to consume her body or to ignore its presence feels like an impossible mission.

The traumatic death of my husband has divided my heart and that of my friends and family. His abuse of Grace and other children is the ever present slur on our relationship and my ability to openly grieve. It has put into the shadows the happy memories and shattered the romantic illusion some hold of the young widow they see before them. I have often felt I am forced to live a duplicit life; a romanticised version of events rather than the whole ugly truth: Mark was a paedophile who abused our own child and others, and then he died. People might prefer not to hear that version of my story. It is difficult to digest and to know what to say in response.

When I have been open about what happened, I have been criticised for not being angry enough or for showing too much compassion; when I have sought to tell my story, some have suggested that I have put my children at risk and the secret is better kept – it is safer not to acknowledge the elephant in the room for fear of the harm she might cause as she runs aground. The events of the last ten years have overwhelmed me just like the shadow of an ever-present elephant in a very tight room. Yet I knew from the beginning of this experience, I would tell my story; I had to break free from these constraints and reach out to others who may have similar elephants in their lives and warn those who may feel exempt from such danger in their own lives of the very significant trappings which occur when you least expect them.

And so I have, with a very small spoon, whittled away at my metaphorical elephant and avoided the temptation to dig one very large hole in which to bury her. I have laid open, consumed, digested, and eventually found some peace in the story I have told, what remains of my beast has in time provided well-trodden and fertile ground to grow new life.

And now as I come to the final chapter, the idea of an elephant graveyard, although largely mythical in nature, sits in my mind's eye. I sense a very spiritual place. A cathedral-like rib cage sits proud and indestructible on a near horizon. In the variable times of day and night this frame casts light and shadow on its arid ground. A permanent presence has formed that will not decay for many years, although eventually it will re-join, as small particles, the sand upon which it stood.

So it is with my story, the shadows have been recounted here; the trauma and the loss will not simply disappear. They too are a great bare-boned structure which sits on the horizon of my life. They cannot be buried deep in sand but are part of the landscape. The dark and the light come and go with variable intensity. And yet, it is the light that draws me in and provides a spiritual sense of peace. And believe me, there is light.

The last nine years have been a time of growth, redirection and change in my life. I would not wish to go through this trauma again. But I know that I would not be the person I am today if I had not endured and begun to master this chapter in my life. I have learnt so much about myself and human kind. I am able to bring this to my work, to the bedside of people who are facing their greatest challenge in life. Although, it has been tempting at times to share my story with the patients or their loved ones that I meet, I have found that I do not need to. It seems I do not need to speak for them to know I understand.

A year ago, an elderly man was admitted to the hospice with severe pain. He had very advanced prostate cancer with secondaries in his bones. He had become very withdrawn and depressed. He told me how a few years earlier his son had committed suicide. In a very intimate consultation, he shared a little of his soul with me and for the first time spoke of how he had found his son and the unrelenting and isolating grief that had ensued. In that moment that we shared, he was able to open up and speak of his trauma with another human being for the first time; he had not even been able to speak of his feelings of despair with his wife. I cried as he told me his story and we were united in our tears. I am not sure how to account for what happened but I do feel there was a connection that went beyond words.

Similarly, on a first home visit, a young woman described to me her world imploding when her husband committed suicide just days before she received the devastating news that her breast cancer had returned and was now untreatable. Again, I did not need to tell her that I knew what it was like to feel this life explosion; to feel like you were in that terrifying place beyond the trenches. Again, somehow our connection went beyond the need to explain.

Perhaps that saddest connection was when an elderly man was admitted to the hospice. He was a retired headmaster who had been married for over sixty years. A frail shell of a man, when you stood at the threshold of his room he seemed to project a sense of gentility and decorum. His wife sat at his bedside when, with the balm of sedation after several weeks of delirious torment, he lay peaceful for his final hours.

But in his confused state stark contradictions had emerged; he had become an animal of a man. Uncharacteristic swear words tumbled across his lips and disturbing pictures of another world were projected into the room. He ranted thoughts of shame and penitence for the things he had been a part of: the conjecture from his ramblings was that he had either abused the children in his care or ignored the actions of those under his charge. To many of the hospice staff, this was a repugnant deathbed confessional.

As the lead clinician, I felt under a lot of pressure from the distressed team to report the crimes they seemed to have heard. We treated his pain and agitation. He quietened and we were hopeful that his delirious tirade had ground to a halt as his wife arrived. But we could not be sure. We did not know if she had experienced similar rambling of thought at home, nor how much she could clarify of the conclusions that had been drawn.

I diverted her to our quiet area before she could reach her husband's room. After I had explained cautiously some of the events overnight and that he was now in his final hours, I tried gently to explore their lives together and her emerging grief. She wept for the man she loved. She seemed to be trying too hard to convince me of how dedicated he had been to his life's work; adding that many of his former students still fondly visited them both at their home. I dug a little deeper; they had never had children: he couldn't. She said no more. She perhaps had chosen not to know why he struggled to consummate their marital bed; they had been a young couple in a time when such things were rarely spoken of within a marriage. But there seemed to be many red flags for those who stood outside the sacred confines of their long relationship. Perhaps her tears gave something away, more than the loss of a husband and sixty years with the same man. For the nurses, who felt they had heard his confessions, it seemed all too clear. But for his wife to be honest with others came at the hefty price of being honest with herself after years of deception. Her misgivings were enough of a torment; I did not challenge her conceivable denial. She needed compassion as she grieved her version of the man she loved. It was too late for confrontation. My heart sank as I thought of my own reality and why I felt both respect and regret for this elderly woman.

I have been working in palliative care for over fifteen years, and I feel I have so much more to give. I am very fortunate to have a vocation that helps me feel I can transcend my loss.

Transcendence is about changes that occur because of losses you have experienced. It is about taking the shattered pieces of your life and making something good but different from them. My favourite bible passage is in 2 Corinthians. Paul describes us as fragile broken jars of clay from which, when pieced back together, light can shine through all the cracks. The light is of God; his goodness is what remains of the breaks.

Friendships have been a cornerstone in reconstructing our lives. I have been so fortunate to have friends who have stood with me. They have been practical and compassionate in their resourcefulness. I have learnt to be more open in my needs. It is immensely challenging and yet edifying to ask for help. This friendship does not mean that at times I don't still feel terribly alone or sad. Their blessings have helped me to acknowledge that I am healing but will never be fully healed. I am able to accept a certain amount of vulnerability with their ongoing support. They are able to allow themselves to be more vulnerable with me. Kitchen table conversations have passed which have created connections that will endure time and distance. Friends have helped me to see light when darkness overshadows.

It might seem impossible to imagine that something good could come out of Mark's actions. After my journey back to the roadside where Mark had died, I was drawn with an insatiable need to search for more detail about the other victim of the crash, any connections Mark might have had with other paedophiles in our home area, and any publicity that might have been drawn from his case. I felt desperate to know more. Because Mark had died in a very rural part of the state, indeed in the middle of nowhere, the accident appears to have drawn no media attention at all. And just as the inspector and trooper had promised, there was no mention of Mark in any media reports of child pornography. I found a Facebook listing for the survivor of the crash but went no further. I am not on Facebook and cannot imagine ever joining. But my search went on, and with relative ease I did stumble upon the unfathomable light in this story. Some incredible good had come out of all this mess.

In 2010, state, national and international press reported that a large child pornography network had been brought down by a single weak link. The coincidences were so striking; it was hard for me to fathom why I had come across these reports without there being some greater purpose. The timing and circumstances seemed uncannily similar to Mark's story.

It was reported that in late 2007 after a man, who was the target of another investigation, gave US postal inspection services consent to use his electronic accounts, authorities had discovered a major international child pornography forum. The authorities took over his email and online identity and used it to access the website. Investigators were then able to follow clues to computers across the globe, including hard drives. The site worked with a hierarchy. Members joined by invitation only and had to be vetted by senior members. Only the most trusted members controlled a huge stash of child pornography. The most severe images were guarded by the forum's very structured hierarchical access and security measures. By February 2008 the authorities had seized the website and in September 2008 it was shut down for good. The forum had over 1,000 members. In the two years that followed this initial lead, many of the senior members and the ringleaders have been arrested. Inspector Hutton had told me that there had been arrests as a direct result of access to Mark's internet identity. I am sure that this media story is Mark's. There are too many similarities: the same location, timing and the details fit. Here is the light in the darkness. I want to believe that this informant was Mark and some good came from all the bad. One such good, from Mark's surrender and ultimately his death, was this domino effect. In reality, it does not matter if I have this wrong because believing it myself gives me some hope.

Traffic in online child pornography has exploded as we have become an internet-centric international society. Children who are abused by online paedophiles are first desensitised to images of other children before being encouraged to act out what they see on screen. The practicalities of the grooming process are shared among forum members, a group culture encourages those who subscribe to generate their own images which they can then upload and share with the forum community. They provide morale and internally legitimise each other's actions. Those who give to the system are rewarded.

Those prosecuted for viewing and distributing such images receive far shorter sentences than those who go beyond the 'virtual abuse' of children. As yet, there remains a poor understanding of the relationship between looking at child pornography and sexually assaulting children. Some who have been prosecuted admit that viewing spurs action, or acknowledge that it has activated latent, sometimes unconscious, desires. It is important that those who work in this field establish a better understanding of offenders and their behaviour. This work is vital to ensuring due thought is given to the appropriate punishment and treatment of those prosecuted.

Our response to paedophiles tends to be reactive and filled with disgust. Sweeping simplification, generalisations and taboos abound. I have even read slurs in online media reports on those who have dared to live with and marry a paedophile; such women are considered by some to be no less a monster or leper than the man they married. As a woman who did marry a paedophile, these comments are extremely upsetting. But I recognise that they do not speak with any knowledge of who I am and my experience. I have learnt to tolerate the arm's length at which people want to hold this topic, the safe and 'comfy' notion that this does not happen in their respectable segment of society. The light for me has been that I have grown so much in my own understanding of crimes against children and those who commit them and no longer see this as someone else's problem. It is our whole society's responsibility and we must act.

As parents, we spend a lot of time creating a safe and secure world for our children. Confidence, energy and love exuded from Grace's carefree dancing and dress up. One day in 2006, life as we knew it changed and we will never be able to go back to the world she once knew. Grace is lucky because she is what they call a 'rescued child'. It is terrible to think that many have been less fortunate. Grace, I hope, will know that she has all the love and support we can muster to help her master her trauma. Both of my children have perhaps learnt too soon that life is not fair; death has cast its shadow very early in their lives, but what shines through is their resilience and determination to move forward. In time, I hope they will forgive and be able to appreciate that their father was not one thing or another; he loved and hurt; he knew the wrong but excused himself from doing what was right. He died knowing the irretrievable mistakes he had made. It is a challenge to keep all the 'versions of Daddy' present and in balance. The inevitable cost seems to be some of sort of cancerous carnage which allows the bad to destroy any memory of the good.

I laboured for over twenty hours when Grace was born. She came out with a strident cry, and it feels as if she has been singing a song ever since. I think of her as my little nightingale; she loves to sing – it is her 'thing'. When I hear her, there is resilience, confidence and beauty in her voice. There is sureness to a sound that I hear nowhere else. As an onlooker, it seems that music has become her vehicle for expressing her feelings; sometimes this moves at a subconscious level. There have been very few opportunities to hear her tell her story but sometimes lyrics seem to do this for me. As she sings 'Safe and Sound', a lyrical Taylor Swift song and backdrop for the movie The Hunger Games, I cannot help but see how the promises in each of its lines resonate with our own lives as she soars through the top notes: there is a promise of a new day as the sun sets; in the dark and the light Grace will be protected; no one can hurt her now. She will be alright. Resilience is indeed her resounding song.

Writing this book has been a challenge. The story of course is not finished, but telling it has been my saving grace. Words on the page have been my own vehicle to say everything I wanted to, about a topic and experience that many cannot find words to express. The paragraphs have helped to clarify and give context to both the trauma and my recovery. The empty page has provided the essential space, free of other opinions and judgement.

If there is a conclusion to be made it is that love, in its many forms, can ultimately transcend this messy story. If I allow myself, I can still remember the man who stood in the dusty Cairo streets protecting me from a devious Bedouin, the man who made me laugh by dressing up as my very own superhero – 'Cough Suppressor Man' – or quite simply the man who held me securely in his arms when I learnt my father was going to die from lung cancer. I can allow myself to remember the Daddy who fearlessly lifted his giggly little girl into the air to 'touch the sky'. In my darker times, I find great comfort in the love shared with my two young children who have the makings of confident, resourceful and resilient young adults.

I remain a hopeless romantic. I hold on to the capacity to love and be loved. And just maybe my next book will be a novel, about a girl who meets a guy in a bookshop.

REFERENCES, RESOURCES
AND ACKNOWLEDGEMENTS

REFERENCES

The poem on p12 is 'The Peace of Wild Things' by Wendell Berry. Copyright © 2012 by Wendell Berry, from New Collected Poems. Reprinted by permission of Counterpoint.

Rabbi Harold S. Kushner, When Bad Things Happen to Good People, reprint edn, Anchor, 2004

www.mayoclinic.org: http://www.mayoclinic.org/diseases-conditions/post-traumatic-stress-disorder/basics/definition/con-20022540

Pat Schwiebert, Tear Soup: A Recipe for Healing After Loss, 5th edition, Grief Watch, 2005

Norman H. Wright, Matt Wooley and Julie Woodley, Surviving the Storms of Life, 2008, Revell Baker Publishing Group

RESOURCES

Lifecentre

Specialises in counselling survivors of rape and sexual violation, whether this has been a recent incident or historical.

www.lifecentre.uk.com

MOSAC

A London-based charity supporting mothers of sexually abused children.

www.mosac.org.uk

WAY

Aims to provide peer-to-peer emotional and practical support to young widowed men and women – married or not, with or without children, whatever their sexual orientation – as they adjust to life after the death of their partner.

www.widowedandyoung.org.uk

ACKNOWLEDGEMENTS

Words are not enough to thank the family, friends and colleagues who supported me through such a difficult season of my life: I am forever grateful to you for your love and tender care.

Thank you mum for giving me the space and time I needed to write. You understood I was compelled to write from the moment the reality of Mark's actions hit home. Your dedication to me and to the children is second to none – you are one in a million. Love really has seen us through.

This book would never have been published without the encouragement all the way along by my dear friend, Sue and my small but cherished writers group.

Thank you Andrew: Andrew Lownie, my agent, came recommended to me, at a writers' festival, as a champion of memoir. When he said yes to my book it felt like more serendipity and, although there have been many dips in the road to publication, Andrew did not give up and believed I had a story worth hearing in my own voice, despite my novice status as a writer. Thank you to Mirror Books for publishing my book; to Jo and Paula, whose team nurtured me through this process until I held my first copy in my hands and wept. You understood how vulnerable I felt when first handing my story over to a complete stranger and allowing them a window into our lives. Thank you Charlotte and Jo for your editorial skill and thoughtfulness; you understood the message I wanted to write and the importance it holds in my life.

Thank you Wendell Berry for your magnificent poem; and Lifecentre, for counsellors like Sue, who is compassionate, skilled and a wonderful listener.

There are many whose names have been changed in this book, but believe me your names are forever engraved in my soul. You stood with me in some of the darkest times, sacrificed some of yourself and helped us find a way to carry on.

I sincerely hope, my children, you will feel between the words on these pages how great my love is for you and my gratitude that you gave me a reason to live. Our healing goes on and I will never stop in my efforts to nurture you through the love and pain.

Thank you, reader. If any among you have taken even one bite of a similar elephant, I wrote this for you and know only this, you can eat an elephant so long as you have the right tools. With my pen and paper in hand I can myself discern what a blessing it has been to be so wonderfully equipped.

Also by Mirror Books

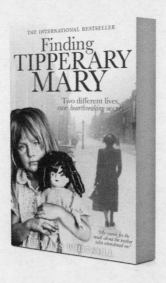

THE INTERNATIONAL BESTSELLER

Finding Tipperary Mary

Phyllis Whitsell

The astonishing real story of a daughter's search for her own past and the desperate mother who gave her up for adoption.

Phyllis Whitsell began looking for her birth mother as a young woman and although it was many years before she finally met her, their lives had crossed on the journey without their knowledge. When they both eventually sat together in the same room, the circumstances were extraordinary, moving and ultimately life-changing.

This is a daughter's personal account of the remarkable relationship that grew from abandonment into love, understanding and selfless care.

Also by Mirror Books

Camera Girl
Doreen Spooner with Alan Clark

The true story of a woman coping with a tragic end to the love of her life and a daily fight to work and support her children.

A moving and inspiring memoir of Doreen Spooner – a woman ahead of her time. Struggling to hold her head high through the disintegration of the family she loves through alcoholism, she began a career as Fleet Street's first female photographer.

While the passionate affair and family life she'd always dreamed of fell apart, Doreen walked into the frantic world of a national newspaper. Determined to save her family from crippling debt, her work captured the Swinging Sixties through political scandals, glamorous stars and cultural icons, while her homelife spiralled further out of control.

The two sides of this book take you through a touching and emotional love story, coupled with a hugely enjoyable portrait of post-war Britain.

Mirror Books

Also by Mirror Books

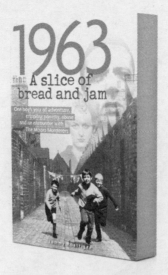

1963 - A Slice of Bread and Jam
Tommy Rhattigan

Tommy lives at the heart of a large Irish family in derelict Hulme in Manchester, ruled by an abusive and alcoholic father. Alongside his siblings he begs (or steals) a few pennies to bring home and avoid a beating, while looking for a little adventure along the way.

His foul-mouthed and chaotic family may be deeply flawed, but amongst the violence, grinding poverty and distinct lack of hygiene and morality lies a strong sense of loyalty and, above all, survival.

During this single year – before his family implodes and his world changes for ever – Tommy almost falls foul of the welfare officers, nuns, police – and Myra Hindley and Ian Brady. An adventurous, fun, dark and moving story of the only life young Tommy knew.